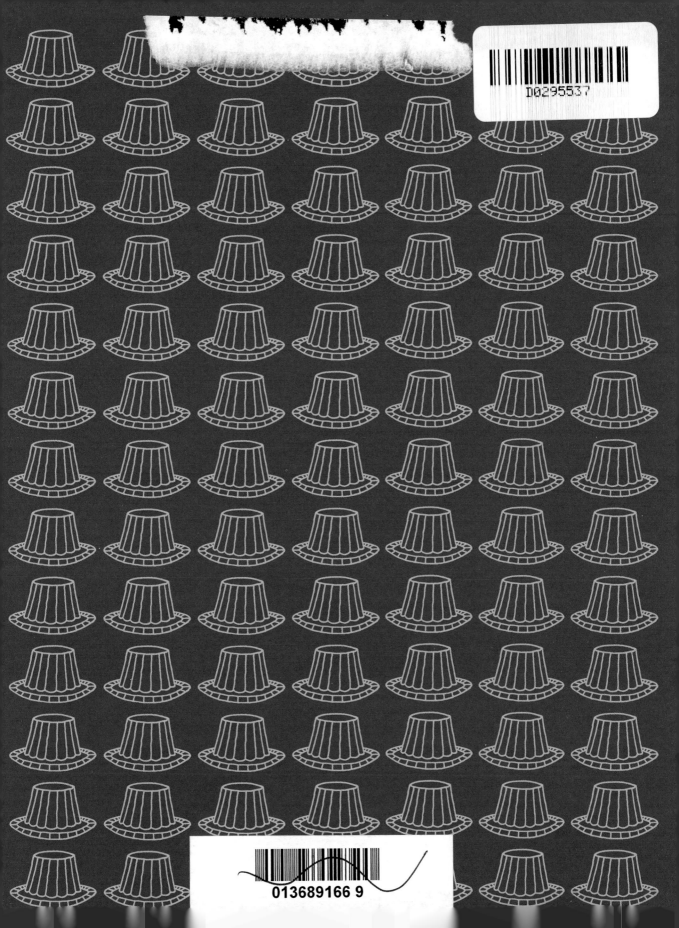

GOOD OLD-FASHIONED

Puddings

GOOD OLD-FASHIONED
Puddings

Sara Paston-Williams

 National Trust

First published in Great Britain in 1983 by David & Charles under the title *The National Trust Book of Traditional Puddings*. New editions published in 2002 and 2007 by National Trust Enterprises Limited

This edition published in the United Kingdom in 2012 by
National Trust Books
10 Southcombe Street
London W14 0RA

An imprint of Anova Books Ltd

ISBN-13 9781907892349

A CIP catalogue record for this book is available from the British Library.

20 19 18 17 16 15 14 13 12
10 9 8 7 6 5 4 3 2 1

Reproduction by Mission Productions Ltd, Hong Kong
Printed and bound by Toppan Leefung Printing Ltd, China

Design by Rosamund Saunders
Food photography by Tara Fisher
Home Economy by Jane Suthering
Styling by Wei Tang

This book can be ordered direct from the publisher at the website: www.anovabooks.com, or try your local bookshop. Also available at National Trust shops or www.shop.nationaltrust.org.uk.

Contents

Introduction

Blessed be he that invented pudding! For it is manna that hits the palates of all sortes of people, better even than that of the wilderness. Ah! what an excellent thing is an English pudding! To come in pudding-time is as much as to say to come in the most lucky moment in the world.

THIS WAS WRITTEN by a Monsieur Misson de Valbourg, a French visitor to Britain in 1690. Another visitor, an Italian, around the same time wrote home saying 'English pies and puddings are literally stuffed with dried fruits and no-one who has not seen it with his own eyes could possibly believe what an incredible number of such pies and puddings the average Englishman is capable of eating!'

The British tradition for delicious puddings is centuries old. Puddings – pies, trifles, fools, flummeries, betties and tarts – have all been served regularly since medieval times. From the earliest recipes, through elaborate Elizabethan and Stuart confections to the elegant 18th- and substantial 19th-century puddings, a tradition has evolved which is an integral part of Britain's culinary heritage.

Almost all British puddings (and here, as in the rest of the book, I am using the word to describe any dish served at the sweet course) have descended from two medieval dishes: the early cereal 'pottage', which was a kind of porridge with honey, wild fruits, shredded meat or fish added to make it more palatable, and 'frumenty', a milk pudding made from wheat or barley and eaten with milk and honey on festive occasions. Originally, puddings such as brightly coloured spiced jellies, flummeries, syllabubs, various tarts, custards, junkets and fruit dishes formed part of a second or third course of a meal, served alongside chicken and fish dishes. A typical second course might consist of veal, sweetbreads, lobster, apricot tart and, in the middle of the table, a pyramid of syllabubs and jellies. In Tudor and Stuart times a special course of sweetmeats known as a 'banquet' became fashionable among the rich.

The enormous variety of puddings and the rapidity with which they were developed in the 17th and 18th centuries, as sugar became cheaper and more available to everyone, show that they filled a real need in the British people's diet – rich in fat and carbohydrates to keep out the cold, and in sugar and fruit to build up energy. The puddings of country folk were often made from meal of cheaper local grains such as oats and barley rather than wheat, but they were just as satisfying.

British cooking has always been influenced by its monarchs and our puddings are no exception. Elizabeth I received annually 'a great pye of quinces, oringed' from her master of the pastry at New Year celebrations. George I was known as 'Pudding George' and is probably the Georgie Porgie mentioned in the well-known nursery rhyme. He, followed by George II and III, loved fattening, suety boiled puddings and dumplings which were devoured all over the kingdom. It was also quite common to see plum duffs and currant dumplings being sold in the streets of London for a halfpenny each.

With the French Revolution came a great transformation in British cooking. Many French chefs fled to Britain and a change of fashion in court circles resulted in the vogue for employing them. Antonin Carême, who worked for the Emperor Napoleon, was lured to Britain to work for the Prince Regent. Queen Victoria employed a number of French chefs, the most famous being Francatelli, who created puddings which we still know – Queen's Pudding, Her Majesty's Pudding, Empress Pudding and Albert Pudding. This fashion was soon copied by a growing and increasingly prosperous middle class who, socially aspiring, encouraged their cooks to make French dishes or, failing that, simply to give French names to traditional British ones. Many of the most delicious and subtle puddings of Georgian times were temporarily forgotten, giving way to rather heavy nursery-style puddings influenced by the German taste of Prince Albert.

Growing literacy had a tremendous influence on cookery. It allowed people, especially women, to write down their favourite recipes, including regional dishes. Many of the traditional pudding recipes were preserved in rural areas, particularly in the large country houses. In towns, speciality restaurants, gentlemen's clubs and grill rooms of the more exclusive hotels continued to serve truly British puddings, so that many recipes have survived, although not always in their original form. In recent years, British food has enjoyed a well-deserved revival, with more and more hotels and restaurants serving our great national dishes and regional specialities. Puddings are a great attraction. Although some are inclined to be rich and fattening, they are homely and delicious and make a lovely treat. Despite our modern obsession with calories, 'pudding-time' still brings murmurs of delight from guests as they tuck into a syrup sponge or plum crumble. Our traditional puddings are glorious – rich and indulgent and comforting. Naughty? Yes, but oh so nice!

Note:
If you want to be a little less indulgent, yoghurt and crème fraîche can be used instead of cream in most recipes, or half and half.

Vegetarian alternatives:
Vegetarian suet and the vegetarian equivalent of lard can be used wherever a recipe includes suet or lard. In fact, I prefer to use vegetarian suet as it gives a lighter finish. Vegetarian setting agents can also be used in place of gelatine, however you must follow the manufacturer's instructions closely.

Conversions

Weight	Liquid measure	Length	Temperature
15g (½oz)	15ml (½fl oz)	5mm (¼in)	110°C (225°F, Gas mark ¼)
25g (1oz)	30ml (1fl oz)	1cm (½in)	120°C (250°F, Gas mark ½)
40g (1½oz)	50ml (2fl oz)	1.5cm (⅜in)	140°C (275°F, Gas mark 1)
50g (1¾oz)	75ml (2½fl oz)	2cm (¾in)	150°C (300°F, Gas mark 2)
55g (2oz)	90ml (3fl oz)	2.5cm (1in)	160°C (325°F, Gas mark 3)
70g (2½oz)	100ml (3½fl oz)	5cm (2in)	180°C (350°F, Gas mark 4)
85g (3oz)	125ml (4fl oz)	7cm (2¾in)	190°C (375°F, Gas mark 5)
100g (3½oz)	150ml (5fl oz or ¼ pint)	9cm (3½in)	200°C (400°F, Gas mark 6)
115g (4oz)	200ml (7fl oz or ⅓ pint)	10cm (4in)	220°C (425°F, Gas mark 7)
125g (4½oz)	250ml (9fl oz)	13cm (5in)	230°C (450°F, Gas mark 8)
140g (5oz)	300ml (10fl oz or ½ pint)	15cm (6in)	240°C (475°F, Gas mark 9)
150g (5½oz)	350ml (12fl oz)	18cm (7in)	
175g (6oz)	400ml (14fl oz)	20cm (8in)	
200g (7oz)	425ml (15fl oz or ¾ pint)	23cm (9in)	
225g (8oz)	450ml (16fl oz)	25cm (10in)	
250g (9oz)	500ml (18fl oz)	28cm (11in)	
300g (10½oz)	600ml (20fl oz or 1 pint)	30cm (12in)	
350g (12oz)	850ml (1½ pint)		
375g (13oz)	1.2l (2 pint)		
400g (14oz)	1.3l (2¾ pint)		
425g (15oz)	1.5l (2¼ pint)		
450g (1lb)			
600g (1lb 5oz)			
675g (1½lb)			
700g (1lb 9oz)			
900g (2lb)			
1kg (2lb 4oz)			

These approximate conversions are used throughout this book.

American Equivalents

Dry measure		
1 US cup	50g (1¾oz)	breadcrumbs; cake crumbs
1 US cup	85g (3oz)	porridge or rolled oats
1 US cup	90g (3¼oz)	ground almonds; shredded coconut
1 US cup	100g (3½oz)	roughly chopped walnuts and other nuts; icing sugar; cocoa; drinking chocolate; flaked almonds; grated Cheddar cheese
1 US cup	150g (5½oz)	white flour; currants; rice flour; muesli; cornflour; chopped dates
1 US cup	175g (6oz)	wholemeal flour; oatmeal; raisins; sultanas; dried apricots; mixed candied peel
1 US cup	200g (7oz)	caster sugar; soft brown sugar; demerara sugar; rice; glacé cherries; semolina; chopped figs or plums
1 US cup	225g (8oz)	granulated sugar; curd cheese; cream cheese
1 US cup	300g (10½oz)	mincemeat; marmalade; jam
1 US cup	350g (12oz)	golden syrup; black treacle

Liquid measures		
⅛ US cup	30ml (1fl oz)	
¼ US cup	50ml (2fl oz)	
½ US cup	125ml (4fl oz)	
1 US cup	250ml (9fl oz)	
1¼ US cups	300ml (10fl oz)	
1¾ US cups	425ml (15fl oz)	
2 US cups	500ml (18fl oz)	
2½ US cups	600ml (20fl oz)	

Measures for fats		
¼ stick	25g (1oz)	
1 stick (½ US cup)	100g (3½oz)	

Baked Puddings

Apple & Marmalade Charlotte

Apple Charlotte was appearing in recipe books by the beginning of the 19th century, filled with 'apple marmalade' (apples cooked in butter, sugar and spices, then beaten to a pulp). This delicious recipe was given to me by the pastry chef at Christ's College, Cambridge, and can be made in a charlotte mould, round cake tin, loaf tin or individual dariole moulds.

serves
6

225g (8oz) butter
115g (4oz) caster sugar
slices of day-old white bread
600g (1lb 5oz) cooking apples

70g (2½oz) fresh white
   breadcrumbs
½ jar good-quality orange
   marmalade
1 tablespoon water

Melt the butter and brush the inside of your chosen mould, then coat with some of the caster sugar. Remove the crusts from the slices of bread (their number will depend on your mould), then dip one slice in the melted butter and place in the bottom of the mould.

Cut some slices of bread in half lengthways, then dip in butter and arrange overlapping each other to line the sides of your mould, taking care not to leave any gaps for the fruit to seep through.

Peel, core and cut the apples into thick slices, and three parts cook in a little butter and sugar. Add the breadcrumbs and about 1 tablespoon of the marmalade. Fill the centre of the mould with the fruit mixture, pressing it down well and giving the mould a bang on the table to release any air.

Place a whole, crustless slice of bread, dipped in the remaining melted butter on the top of the apples and bake in a preheated oven at 220°C (425°F, Gas mark 7) for 30–40 minutes or until brown.

Remove from the oven, and take off the piece of bread on the top. Trim around the edge of the mould with a sharp knife, then turn out on to a warm serving plate. Melt the remaining marmalade with the water, over a low heat, then pour over the charlotte.

Apple Dappy

A traditional Victorian recipe from the West Country, where apples were grown in vast quantities for eating and for cider-making.

serves
4–6

for the lemon syrup
1 large lemon
1 tablespoon golden syrup
15g (½oz) butter
115g (4oz) caster sugar
200ml (7fl oz) water

for the pudding
225g (8oz) self-raising flour
1 level teaspoon baking powder
55g (2oz) butter, cut in small pieces
150ml (¼ pint) milk
450g (1lb) cooking apples
1 tablespoon demerara sugar
½ teaspoon ground cinnamon
   or allspice

Preheat the oven to 190°C (375°F, Gas mark 5). To make the lemon syrup, peel the lemon as thinly as possible and squeeze out the juice. Place the lemon rind, juice and all the other ingredients, into a pan and heat gently, stirring until the sugar is dissolved. Leave to stand until needed.

Sieve the flour and baking powder into a large mixing bowl and rub in the butter until the mixture resembles breadcrumbs. Mix to a dough with the milk, then roll out on a floured board to about 20cm (8in) square and approximately 5mm (¼in) thick.

Peel, core and chop the apples, then spread on the pastry. Sprinkle with the sugar and spice and roll up like a Swiss roll. Cut into 2.5cm (1in) slices and arrange in a buttered 1.2 litre (2 pint) ovenproof dish.

Strain the lemon rind from the prepared syrup and pour the liquid over the pudding. Bake for about 30 minutes, or until puffed up and golden. Serve hot with clotted cream.

Apple Cobs

Also known as Bomdard'd Apples or Apple Dumplings. In the original recipe the dumplings were boiled, but here they are baked. Use a really good-quality cooking apple that will go soft and puffy when cooked. You can use shortcrust or puff pastry instead of suet-crust pastry if you want a less rich pudding.

serves 6

350g (12oz) self-raising flour
pinch of salt
175g (6oz) suet
50g (1¾oz) caster sugar
about 150ml (¼ pint) ice-cold water
6 medium Bramley apples

2 tablespoons mincemeat
6 cloves
water or milk for brushing
1 egg white, beaten
3 tablespoons clotted cream
  (optional)

Sieve the flour and salt together into a mixing bowl. Mix in the suet and stir in half the sugar. Add just sufficient water to mix to a soft but not sticky dough. Turn out on to a lightly floured board and divide into 6 equal pieces. Roll out each piece thinly into a square large enough to encase an apple.

Peel and core the apples and place one in the centre of each pastry square. Fill each apple centre with mincemeat and top with a clove. Brush the edge of each pastry square with a little water or milk, draw up the corners to meet over the centre of each apple and press the edges firmly together. Turn upside down, and place on a greased baking tray. Roll out the pastry trimmings to make small leaves to decorate the dumplings, then brush all over with the egg white and sprinkle with the remaining sugar.

Bake in the centre of a preheated oven at 200°C (400°F, Gas mark 6) for 30 minutes or until golden brown. Remove from the oven and leave to stand for a few minutes on a warm serving dish. Cut a hole in the top of each dumpling and spoon in some clotted cream, or serve with Vanilla Custard Sauce (see page 207).

Nottingham Pudding

Also known as Apple-In-and-Out, this pudding is a combination of apple and batter, dating back to medieval days when dried fruits, spices and candied peel were put in a batter pudding and served with joints of meat. This tradition has continued in the north of England, where any leftovers are served after the meal with melted butter and treacle, lemon juice and sugar or warmed honey and cinnamon.

<table>
<tr><td>serves
4–6</td><td>115g (4oz) plain flour
pinch of salt
1 large egg
150ml (¼ pint) full-cream milk
150ml (¼ pint) water
450g (1lb) cooking apples</td><td>40g (1½oz) butter
zest of ½ lemon
½ teaspoon ground cinnamon
70g (2½oz) soft brown sugar
40g (1½oz) margarine</td></tr>
</table>

Sieve the flour and salt together into a basin and make a well in the centre. Break the egg into the well and stir to mix with the flour. Gradually add half the milk and water, beating well with a wooden spoon until the batter is smooth and creamy. Add the remaining liquid, beating with a rotary or electric whisk to keep the batter smooth and light. Leave to stand in a cool place for about 30 minutes.

Peel, core and slice the apples. Melt the butter in a heavy frying pan, add the apples, lemon zest, cinnamon and sugar, cover and cook gently until the apples are just tender.

Put the margarine in a 19cm (7½in) square baking tin and heat near the top of a preheated oven at 220°C (425°F, Gas mark 7) until the fat is smoking. Remove from the oven and carefully add the apple mixture and pour the batter over. Return to the oven for about 20 minutes, then reduce the temperature to 190°C (375°F, Gas mark 5) for a further 20–25 minutes or until the batter is firm and golden brown (this batter pudding will not rise as much as a Yorkshire pudding, because of the fruit it contains).

Mother Eve's Pudding

Traditionally made with tempting apples under a sponge topping, hence the name! However, you can use any fruit and the flavourings can be varied accordingly by adding spices or orange zest. The Georgian recipe for this pudding was made with suet and included currants as well as the apples. It was also boiled rather than baked.

serves
6

600g (1lb 5oz) cooking apples
85g (3oz) caster sugar
zest of 1 lemon
2 cloves
1 tablespoon water
115g (4oz) salted butter

115g (4oz) caster sugar
2 eggs
¼ teaspoon vanilla extract
115g (4oz) self-raising flour
1 tablespoon warm water
caster sugar for dredging

Butter a 1.2 litre (2 pint) ovenproof dish. Peel, core and slice the apples thinly and place in a heavy saucepan with the sugar, lemon zest, cloves and water. Heat over gentle heat for a few minutes until just tender. Turn into the prepared dish and leave to cool.

Cream butter and sugar together in a mixing bowl until pale and fluffy. Beat eggs and add gradually to creamed mixture, beating well after each addition. Beat in the vanilla extract, and gently fold sieved flour into creamed mixture. Stir in warm water to make a soft dropping consistency and spread evenly over apples.

Bake in the centre of a preheated oven at 190°C (375°F, Gas mark 5) for about 45 minutes, or until well risen and golden brown (test with a fine skewer, which should come out clean). Serve hot or cold, dredged with caster sugar and with Vanilla Custard Sauce (see page 207) or Lemon Sauce (see page 210).

Apple & Almond Pudding

Substitute 115g (4oz) ground almonds for self-raising flour and continue as before. Serve hot or cold with pouring cream.

Gingerbread & Pear Upside-down Pudding

This was a popular pudding in Victorian days and looks very attractive. You can bake it in a round or square tin.

serves
6

50g (1¾oz) butter
140g (5oz) soft brown sugar
3 firm pears
6 glacé cherries
6 walnut halves
115g (4oz) margarine
115g (4oz) black treacle
115g (4oz) golden syrup
225g (8oz) plain flour

¼ teaspoon salt
pinch of ground cloves
2 teaspoons ground cinnamon
2 teaspoons ground ginger
¼ teaspoon grated nutmeg
1 level teaspoon bicarbonate of soda
150ml (¼ pint) warm
    full-cream milk
2 eggs

Line the bottom and sides of a 20cm (8in) round cake tin with buttered greaseproof paper. Melt the butter in a saucepan over gentle heat, add 70g (2½oz) brown sugar and stir for a few minutes until dissolved. Pour into the bottom of the tin. Peel, halve and core the pears and put a glacé cherry in the centre of each pear half. Arrange the pears in a circle cut-side down on the butter-and-sugar mixture with stalk ends facing the centre of the tin. Place walnut halves, cut-side down, between the pears.

Put margarine, black treacle, golden syrup and remaining brown sugar in a saucepan and melt over a low heat. Sieve flour, salt and spices together into a mixing bowl. Dissolve soda in warm milk. Beat eggs and add to milk mixture when it has cooled a little. Make a well in the centre of the dry ingredients and pour in melted treacle mixture, followed by egg mixture. Stir together and beat thoroughly until a smooth batter is formed. Pour carefully over the pears and walnuts. Bake in the centre of a preheated oven at 180°C (350°F, Gas mark 4) for 40–50 minutes or until well risen and firm (test with a skewer; it should come out clean). Remove from the oven and allow to shrink a little before turning out on to a warmed serving plate. Take great care when peeling off greaseproof paper. Serve warm with cream or Vanilla Custard Sauce (see page 207).

Plum & Cinnamon Crumble

Crumbles can be varied, not just by using seasonal fruit but also by changing the crumble topping, adding porridge oats (as here), dessicated coconut, chopped nuts, different spices and so on. Classic combinations such as rhubarb and ginger, apple and cinnamon, gooseberry and elderflower, can always be relied on. This particular recipe was given to me by a good friend, who is chef at Cotehele, a medieval house belonging to the National Trust on the banks of the River Tamar, in Cornwall. He cooks the crumble in individual dishes under the grill.

serves
4

600g (1 lb 5oz) English plums, stoned
50g (1¾oz) light brown sugar
½ teaspoon ground cinnamon

for the topping
40g (1½oz) butter, cut in small pieces
55g (2oz) plain flour
1/2 teaspoon cinnamon
40g (1½oz) light brown sugar
55g (2oz) porridge oats

Poach the plums with the sugar and cinnamon and a very little water until just tender. Remove from the heat and tip into a buttered ovenproof baking dish.

Rub the butter into the flour and cinnamon sieved together, into a mixing bowl until the mixture resembles breadcrumbs. Stir in the sugar and oats.

Sprinkle evenly over the plums and bake in a preheated oven at 180°C (350°F, Gas mark 4) for about 25 minutes, or until golden brown. Remove from the oven and leave to cool a little. Eat warm and serve with Vanilla Custard Sauce (see page 207), Vanilla Ice Cream (see page 71) or clotted cream.

Damson Cobbler

This pudding presumably takes its name from the scone topping, which does look rather like cobblestones. You can either cut out dough into circles and place them round the edges of the dish, overlapping each other, or you can lay the dough over like a pie crust and cut it into squares – either way, it is a delicious and economical pudding. Many fruits can be used instead of damsons – plums, greengages, blackcurrants, blackberries, apples, rhubarb, bilberries and gooseberries. This particular recipe is made in Cumbria from local damsons.

serves
6

900g (2lb) damsons
250g (9oz) caster sugar
150ml (¼ pint) water
225g (8oz) self-raising flour
pinch of salt
55g (2oz) butter
1 egg
1–2 tablespoons milk
granulated sugar for sprinkling

Wash the damsons and cook slowly in a heavy saucepan with 225g (8oz) sugar and the water until just tender. Remove the stones and turn into a buttered ovenproof dish. Leave to cool.

Sieve the flour and salt together into a mixing bowl. Stir in the remaining sugar and rub in the butter. Beat the egg and add to the mixture with enough milk to make a soft dough. Roll out on a lightly floured board to about 1cm (½in) thick. Cut out the dough into rounds with a 5cm (2in) cutter and arrange in a ring around the edge of the dish of fruit with the rounds overlapping each other. Brush the scone topping with a little milk, and bake near the top of a preheated oven at 220°C (425°F, Gas mark 7) for 10 minutes. Reduce the oven temperature to 190°C (375°F, Gas mark 5). Sprinkle the top generously with granulated sugar and bake for a further 5–10 minutes until well risen and golden brown.

Lemon Pudding

This lovely pudding is based on a very old recipe which was baked in a dish lined with puff pastry. By whisking egg whites and adding just before baking, the pudding will be very light. You may need to cover with greaseproof paper if the top is getting brown too quickly before the underneath has set. This pudding separates out during cooking into a tangy custard layer with a featherlight sponge topping. An orange or lime pudding can be made in the same way.

serves
4–6

100g (3½oz) butter, softened
175g (6oz) caster sugar
zest and juice of 4 lemons
4 eggs, separated
125ml (4fl oz) full-cream milk
50g (1¾oz) plain flour

Cream the butter and sugar together until white and fluffy, then beat in the lemon zest and juice. Beat the egg yolks into the creamed mixture very gradually. When the mixture is very light, beat in the milk. Fold in the sieved flour.

Whisk the egg whites until they are firm and stand in peaks. Fold them gently into the lemon mixture, then pour into a buttered 20cm (8in) soufflé dish. Place the dish in a roasting tin and pour hot water into the tin until it comes halfway up the sides of the dish.

Bake in the centre of a preheated oven at 180°C (350°F, Gas mark 4), for about 45 minutes, until the top is golden brown and the pudding has risen. Serve warm, or cold with cream.

Rhubarb & Orange Betty

An original 19th-century Brown Betty was made with apples, breadcrumbs and suet and was a popular pudding with lower-paid countryfolk. Delicious Brown Betty can be made with other fruits, but the amount of sugar must be adjusted accordingly. Some of the most successful are rhubarb (as here), plums, gooseberries, damsons, blackcurrants, blackberries and cherries.

serves 4–6

85g (3oz) butter
115g (4oz) fresh white breadcrumbs
450g (1lb) rhubarb
85–115g (3–4 oz) caster or soft brown sugar
zest and juice of 1 orange

Melt the butter in a heavy frying pan, add the breadcrumbs and cook over moderate heat, stirring continuously to prevent burning, until the crumbs are light golden in colour.

Cut the rhubarb into 2.5cm (1in) lengths, then mix with the sugar, orange zest and juice. Butter a 1.2 litre (2 pint) ovenproof dish and fill with alternate layers of rhubarb and breadcrumbs, finishing with a layer of crumbs. Sprinkle with extra sugar and cover with foil. Bake in the centre of a preheated oven at 180°C (350°F, Gas mark 4) for 20 minutes, then remove the foil and continue cooking for a further 25–30 minutes, or until the top is brown and crisp and the rhubarb is lovely and soft. Serve hot with Vanilla Custard Sauce (see page 207) or cream.

Curate's Pudding

This recipe comes from the *The Best of Eliza Acton*, first published in 1845. It's an excellent pudding, best made with seasonal British fruits. I use thinly sliced brioche buns instead of 'penny rolls', but bread rolls or slices of bread work just as well.

serves
4

450g (1lb) young pink rhubarb
25g (1oz) butter
4 tablespoons caster sugar
2 brioche buns, thinly sliced

Cut the rhubarb into 2.5cm (1in) lengths. Melt the butter and brush the insides of a 1.2 litre (2 pint) soufflé dish or ovenproof dish with a little of it. Place half the rhubarb into the dish and sprinkle on about half the sugar. Cover the fruit with a layer of brioche slices.

Now lay on the remaining fruit and sprinkle on all but a teaspoon of the remaining sugar. Cover the rhubarb with slices of brioche, shaping to fit. Press down with your hand to flatten the pudding, then brush the top with the remaining butter. Sprinkle with the remaining sugar and bake in a preheated oven at 180°C (350°F, Gas mark 4) for about 30 minutes, or until the fruit is tender and the top browned. Serve warm with cream.

Cherry Batter

This famous pudding from Kent has been eaten at cherry feasts and fairs since the 13th century, but probably the idea of combining cherries with batter came to the UK with the Normans. This dish is a reminder that Kent was one of the first counties to be colonised by the invaders. Kent's famous juicy black morello cherries, said to be the best black cherries in the world, should be used to make this delicious pud, but drained tinned black cherries can be used out of season.

serves 6

50g (1¾oz) plain flour
pinch of salt
50g (1¾oz) caster sugar
2 eggs
300ml (½ pint) single-
    or full-cream milk

1 tablespoon cherry brandy or
    a few drops of vanilla essence
25g (1oz) melted butter
450g (1lb) ripe black cherries,
    stoned
icing sugar for dredging

Sieve the flour and salt together into a bowl. Stir in the caster sugar. Beat the eggs and blend gradually into flour mixture. Warm the milk and add slowly to the flour mixture beating vigorously to make a smooth light batter. Stir in cherry brandy or vanilla essence and whisk in melted butter. Put aside to rest while you stone the cherries.

Generously butter a shallow 600ml (1 pint) ovenproof porcelain dish or a 20cm (8in) flan tin. Spread the prepared cherries over the bottom of the dish or tin and carefully pour over the batter. Dot with a few tiny pieces of butter and bake in the centre of a preheated oven at 200°C (400°F, Gas mark 6) for 20 minutes, then reduce the temperature to 190°C (375°F, Gas mark 5) and cook for a further 20 minutes or until the batter is well risen and golden, but still creamy inside. Serve warm, generously dredged with sieved icing sugar and with whipped cream or Vanilla Custard Sauce (see page 207). If you want to serve the pudding cold, remove from the dish or tin and serve with either pouring or whipped cream.

Quantock Pudding

Batter puddings similar to the famous French clafoutis used to be made in most fruit growing areas in Britain (see Cherry Batter, page 28). The Quantock or Somerset version used blackberries, but any soft fruits are suitable, such as raspberries and blackberries, as well as apples, pears, rhubarb, apricots and gooseberries.

serves 4–6

50g (1¾oz) butter
55g (2oz) plain flour
4 medium eggs
115g (4oz) caster sugar
1 vanilla pod, split in half lengthways
    and seeds scraped out

1 tablespoon Kirsch
150ml (¼ pint) whipping cream
150ml (¼ pint) full-cream milk
450g (1lb) blackberries
icing sugar to dust

Preheat the oven to 200°C (400°F, Gas mark 6). Using half the butter, liberally grease a shallow gratin, ovenproof baking dish or cast-iron frying pan with 1.2 litre (2 pint) capacity.

In a large bowl, whisk together the flour, eggs, sugar, seeds from the vanilla pod and Kirsch until creamy, then stir in the cream and milk. Strain, if there are any stubborn lumps.

Place the buttered dish in the oven for a couple of minutes until very hot, then remove from the oven. Immediately pour in half of the batter, sprinkle the blackberries on top, then pour over the remaining batter. Dot the remaining butter over the surface, then bake for 30 minutes, or until puffed up and golden brown and a skewer inserted into the mixture comes out completely clean. Leave for at least 20 minutes before serving just warm and dusted with sieved icing sugar. Eat with lightly whipped cream.

Tewkesbury Saucer Batters

Saucers were used for baking small savoury and sweet pies and puddings years before they were used under teacups, and a few recipes still survive. This one comes from Gloucestershire and is for batter puddings baked in saucers. You can serve them filled with fresh soft fruit such as raspberries, blackberries, loganberries or strawberries. They make a very unusual pudding for a dinner party. The quantities given here will make 4 saucer batters, which will be enough for 8 people, but if your guests or family have large appetites and can polish off a saucer batter each, you will have to make more batter!

serves
4–8

225g (8oz) plain flour
¼ teaspoon salt
2 eggs, separated
600ml (1 pint) milk
700g (1lb 9oz) soft fruit
115–175g (4–6oz) caster sugar

Sieve flour and salt together into a mixing bowl. Make a well in the centre and put in egg yolks. Beat in egg yolks gradually, adding milk a little at a time and beating continuously until the mixture becomes a smooth creamy batter. Leave in a cool place for at least 30 minutes, for the starch to begin to break down.

Meanwhile, well butter 4 ovenproof saucers. Put the fruit in an ovenproof dish and sprinkle with sugar, cover and put in the oven while it is heating up until the juices begin to run. Taste to see if sweet enough (be careful not to cook strawberries for more than a few seconds or they will go mushy). Take the fruit from the oven and leave on one side.

Whisk egg whites until very stiff, and fold into the batter. Divide the batter between 4 prepared saucers, and put in the top of a preheated oven at 230°C (450°F, Gas mark 8). Bake for about 15–20 minutes or until golden brown and coming away from the edges of the saucers. Remove from the oven when cooked, and slide on to a warmed serving dish. Sprinkle with caster sugar and fill each batter with fruit. Serve hot with whipped cream.

Apricot Amber Pudding

Traditionally, an Amber Pudding was made with apples and baked in a puff-pastry case. It is a very old-fashioned sweet dating back to the 18th century, and can be made with many other fruits such as apples, rhubarb, gooseberries, blackberries, blackcurrants or plums.

**serves
6**

175g (6oz) shortcrust pastry
450g (1lb) fresh apricots
about 150g (5½oz)
    caster sugar
1 teaspoon lemon juice

25g (1oz) unsalted butter
2 eggs, separated
pinch of salt
crystallized apricot and
    angelica to decorate

Preheat the oven to 200°C (400°C, Gas mark 6), with a large baking sheet in the oven to warm up as well. Roll out the pastry thinly and use to line a buttered 20cm (8in) shallow ovenproof dish. Chill in the refrigerator for 30 minutes. Prick the base and line with baking paper and baking beans. Place in the oven on the hot baking sheet and bake blind for about 10 minutes, then remove the baking parchment and beans and cook for about another 10 minutes to dry out the inside without browning the pastry.

Meanwhile, wash and stone the apricots, then poach in a little water until tender. Rub the fruit through a plastic sieve, then sweeten with about 40g (1½oz) sugar or to taste, adding the lemon juice. Stir in the butter, and beat in the egg yolks. Leave on one side to cool.

Pour the cooled apricot mixture into the cooked pastry case and cook for 20 minutes in the preheated oven at 200°C (400°F, Gas mark 6).

Whisk the egg whites with the salt until stiff, but not dry. Add 55g (2oz) caster sugar and whisk until stiff again. Fold in another 55g (2oz) sugar gently. Reduce the oven temperature to 180°C (350°F, Gas mark 4). Pile the meringue on top of the apricot mixture and spread out, making sure that it touches the edges of the pastry. Dredge with extra caster sugar and bake in the centre of the oven for 20 minutes, or until the meringue is crisp and very lightly browned. Serve warm or cold with whipped cream and decorated with pieces of crystallized apricot and candied angelica, if you wish.

Rich Bakewell Pudding

There are several 'original' recipes in Derbyshire for this famous pudding, but generally it is accepted that it was probably first made by a cook at the Rutland Arms in Bakewell two hundred years ago. The original recipe was made in a special oval tin 7.5cm (3in) deep and 15cm (6in) wide and had a thick layer of preserved fruit, such as peaches or apricots, and strips of candied citron or orange peel spread over the pastry. A custard made with eggs, butter and sugar and flavoured with what the Bakewellians call 'lemon brandy' (brandy flavoured with lemon zest) was poured on top of the preserved fruit and the pudding was baked. Ratafia or almond flavouring is more commonly used now, and flaky or rich shortcrust pastry can be used instead of shortcrust.

serves
6

175g (6oz) shortcrust pastry
3 heaped tablespoons homemade or
   good-quality apricot jam
25g (1oz) candied peel, chopped
3 eggs
115g (4oz) caster sugar

115g (4oz) unsalted butter
½ teaspoon vanilla extract or
   ratafia flavouring
1 tablespoon brandy
115g (4oz) ground almonds
sieved icing sugar for dredging

Roll out the pastry and use to line a buttered 20cm (8in) oval pie dish. Chill, then bake blind in the usual way (see Apricot Amber Pudding, page 32). Spread the jam evenly over the cooled pastry case and sprinkle with the peel.

Beat eggs and sugar together until pale and thick. Melt the butter and run into egg mixture. Beat together well. Stir in vanilla essence or ratafia and brandy. Fold in ground almonds. Pour the mixture over the jam and candied peel in the pastry case. Bake in the centre of the preheated oven at 180°C (350°F, Gas mark 4), for about 30 minutes or until the filling is set and golden brown. Dredge with sieved icing sugar and serve hot, warm or cold with pouring cream.

Jam Roly-Poly

This popular pudding used to be boiled in a cloth or shirtsleeve, but baking gives the pastry a lovely crisp crust which is usually more popular with children. Mincemeat or golden syrup can be used instead of jam.

serves
4–6

225g (8oz) self-raising flour
1 teaspoon mixed spice (optional)
pinch of salt
115g (4oz) suet
about 8 tablespoons water

4–5 tablespoons good-quality
    jam, warmed
milk, for brushing
1 egg, beaten, to glaze
caster sugar for sprinkling

Sieve flour, spice (if using) and salt together into a mixing bowl. Stir in the suet and add just enough water to mix to a soft, but not sticky, dough. Turn out on to a lightly floured board and roll into a rectangle about 20 x 30cm (8 x 12in). Spread evenly with warm jam leaving a 1cm (½in) border all the way around. Fold this border over the jam and brush with milk. Roll up fairly loosely and press the edges of the dough together to seal them. Put in a lightly buttered roasting tin and brush with beaten egg. Sprinkle with caster sugar.

Bake in the centre of a preheated oven at 200°C (400°F, Gas mark 6), with the tin propped up so that the roly-poly rolls into one end, which helps to keep its shape. Cook for 35–40 minutes or until golden brown.

Serve warm, sprinkled with extra caster sugar and Vanilla Custard Sauce (see page 207).

Roly-poly with Blueberries

Make the roly-poly as before, but fill with 300g (10½oz) fresh blueberries mixed with 1 tablespoon flour, 4 tablespoons caster sugar and juice of 1 lemon or lime. Try other seasonal soft fruits and serve with Vanilla Custard Sauce (see page 207), Vanilla Ice Cream (see page 71) or thick cream.

Bread & Butter Pudding

Bread and Butter Pudding was in the recipe books by the 1720s, when it was made of freshly sliced and buttered bread with currants, beaten eggs and nutmeg. It was only in Victorian times that it became a means of putting stale bread to good use. Since then it has become a British institution and there are dozens of versions. Modern recipes sometimes add fresh or poached fruit, marmalade, apricot jam or chocolate and use brioche, fruit loaf, panettone and croissants. I love a Bread and Butter Pudding with a high proportion of rich custard to bread.

serves 6

300ml (½ pint) full-cream or
    Jersey milk
300ml (½ pint) double cream
1 vanilla pod, split in half
    lengthways
4–6 slices cut from a good-quality
    white sandwich loaf

about 100g (3½oz) butter, softened
55g (2oz) sultanas, soaked in hot water
25g (1oz) candied peel, chopped
3 large eggs
about 70g (2½oz) caster sugar
freshly grated nutmeg
icing sugar for dredging

Slowly heat the milk and cream with the vanilla pod, including its scraped-out seeds, until boiling point is just reached. Take off the heat and leave to cool a little.

Remove the crusts from the bread and butter generously. Cut each slice into 4 triangles, then arrange, overlapping in the base of a well-buttered 1.5 litre (2¾ pint) ovenproof dish. Sprinkle with the soaked and drained sultanas and peel.

Whisk the eggs with the sugar, then pour into a jug with the strained milk and cream mixture. Taste and add more sugar, if you wish. Whisk again, then carefully pour evenly over the bread, making sure that each triangle gets a good soaking (add more milk if the liquid doesn't cover the bread). Grate plenty of nutmeg over the surface, cover and leave to soak for at least 2 hours, preferably overnight, in the refrigerator. When ready to cook, place the dish in a roasting tin filled with hot water to the level of the top of the custard.

Bake in a preheated oven at 150°C (300°F, Gas mark 2) for 1–1¼ hours until just set and golden (after 30 minutes cooking time, dredge with icing sugar to crisp up the top). Rest for 20 minutes before serving. No extra cream is really necessary because the custard is very rich and delicious.

Old-fashioned Bread Pud

In Plymouth, this very old pudding is called Nelson's Cake after the great man who was obviously a lover of it. It is also particularly popular in East Anglia, where Nelson was born. The original version would have been boiled but it is now more commonly baked. Individual bread puddings were fashionable in Georgian times – they were baked in buttered teacups.

serves 4

225g (8oz) stale white or brown bread, with crusts removed
300ml (½ pint) milk
2 tablespoons brandy (optional)
50g (1¾oz) melted butter or suet
50g (1¾oz) soft brown sugar
2 level teaspoons mixed spice

1 egg, beaten
175g (6oz) mixed dried fruit
zest of 1 lemon
zest of ½ orange
freshly grated nutmeg
caster sugar for sprinkling

Break the bread into small pieces and put in a mixing bowl. Pour over the milk and brandy, if using, stir well and leave to soak for at least 30 minutes.

Add the melted butter or suet, sugar, spice and egg then, using a fork, beat out any lumps. Stir in the dried fruit and grated lemon and orange zest, then turn the mixture into a buttered 1.2 litre (2 pint) ovenproof dish. Grate a little fresh nutmeg over the top.

Bake in a preheated oven at 180°C (350°F, Gas mark 4) for 1¼–1½ hours until nicely brown on top. Serve hot, sprinkled with caster sugar and with Vanilla Custard Sauce (see page 207).

Old-fashioned Iced Bread Pud

Make as before, but remove from the oven after 1 hour. Cover with meringue made from 2 egg whites and 115g (4oz) caster sugar. Put back in the oven and cook for a further 20 minutes, or until the meringue is crisp and lightly browned.

Hollygog Pudding

This is a golden syrupy roly-poly which is baked in milk. It was first made in the Oxfordshire village of Kiddington, where it has been passed down among farming families.

serves
4–6

225g (8oz) plain flour
pinch of salt
115g (4oz) butter
about 3 tablespoons cold water
4 tablespoons golden syrup, warmed
about 300ml (½ pint) full-cream milk

Sieve the flour and salt into a mixing bowl and rub the fat into the flour until the mixture resembles breadcrumbs. Add water to form a stiff dough. Roll out into a rectangular strip, spread with syrup and roll up like a Swiss roll.

Put in a well-buttered oval ovenproof dish and pour over enough milk to come halfway up the side of the pudding. Bake in a preheated oven at 200°C (400°F, Gas mark 6) for 40–45 minutes.

Serve hot in slices with cream, Economical Custard Sauce (see page 208) or Vanilla Custard Sauce (see page 207).

Icky Sticky Toffee Sponge

A top favourite with most people, the original recipe for this pudding probably dates back to the 1930s. It was made famous in the 1960s by the late great Francis Coulson, chef and proprietor of the Sharrow Bay Country House Hotel in Ullswater, Cumbria.

serves 6–8

for the sponge

50g (1¾oz) butter
175g (6oz) granulated sugar
175g (6oz) dates, stoned and chopped
300ml (½ pint) water
1 teaspoon bicarbonate of soda
2 large eggs
175g (6oz) self-raising flour
a few drops of vanilla extract

for the sauce

40g (1½oz) demerara sugar
1 tablespoon black treacle, golden
  syrup or honey
300ml (½ pint) double cream

To make the sponge, cream the butter and sugar together. Boil the chopped dates in the water for about 10 minutes or until soft, then add the bicarbonate of soda. Beat the eggs into the creamed mixture, followed by the sieved flour, dates, water and vanilla extract. Pour into a buttered 20cm (8in) round, loose-bottomed cake tin that is at least 7.5cm (3in) deep. Bake in a preheated oven at 180°C (350°F, Gas mark 4) for about 40 minutes, or until firm to the touch.

Meanwhile, make the sauce. Put the sugar and treacle in a pan and heat gently, stirring until the sugar has dissolved. Stir in the cream and bring to the boil. Remove from the heat and leave to stand until needed.

When the pudding is cooked, remove from the oven and leave for 5 minutes, then turn out on to a warm serving plate. Pour over the sauce. Put under the grill for a few minutes until the sauce bubbles, then serve with Vanilla Ice Cream (see page 71).

Chocolate Puddle Pudding

A firm family favourite, this pudding emerges from the oven with its own built-in sauce hidden under a layer of chocolate sponge. Its exact origin is vague although it has been around for years.

serves
4–6

for the pudding
115g (4oz) butter, softened
115g (4oz) soft light
    brown sugar
1 teaspoon vanilla extract
2 large eggs, beaten
85g (3oz) self-raising flour
25g (1oz) cocoa powder
a little milk

for the sauce
85g (3oz) light brown sugar
25g (1oz) cocoa powder
300ml (½ pint) full-cream milk

Preheat the oven to 180°C (350°F, Gas mark 4). Cream the butter and sugar together until light and fluffy. Beat in the vanilla extract, then gradually beat in the eggs.

Sieve the flour and cocoa together, then fold into the creamed mixture. Mix in just enough milk to give a soft dropping consistency. Spoon into a buttered 1.2 litre (2 pint) ovenproof dish.

For the sauce, mix the sugar and cocoa together and gradually beat in the milk. Pour evenly over the pudding mixture and bake for 40–60 minutes, or until just set in the centre. (If the pudding is a bit too soft in the centre, the sauce will be thin when you cut into the pudding, but if you overcook so that the pudding is very firm in the centre, the sauce will disappear. The centre should spring back when you press it lightly, with your fingertips.) Leave to stand for 5 minutes, before serving with Vanilla Ice Cream (see page 71) or cream.

Creams, Flummeries, Fools, Snows & Syllabubs

Victorian Apple Snow

This dish of apples and whisked egg whites has ancient ancestors. Egg whites were first beaten in Elizabethan days and used to produce their 'dishful of snow', a spectacular centrepiece for the banquet course following a festive meal. They were beaten with thick cream, rose water and sugar until the froth rose and was gathered in a colander. This was built up over an apple and a bed of rosemary on a platter.

The same dish with the addition of whipped cream continued into the 18th century as Snow Cream or Blanched Cream. Another form with the addition of apple pulp came to be known as Apple Snow and other seasonal fruit pulps were also used. In Victorian times the cream was omitted and became the pudding that we know today.

serves 6

1kg (2lb 4oz) Bramley apples
1 tablespoon lemon juice
3 tablespoons sweet cider or water
zest of 1 lemon
about 85g (3oz) caster sugar

pinch of ground cinnamon (optional)
3 egg whites
about 4 teaspoons golden muscovado sugar, to decorate
edible fresh flowers, to decorate

Peel, core and thinly slice the apples. Put in a heavy saucepan with the lemon juice, cider or water, and lemon zest. Cover and cook over very low heat until quite soft and fluffy, stirring once or twice. Now remove the lid and continue cooking, stirring frequently, until the apples are reduced to a foam and most of the moisture has been driven off. Remove from the heat and stir in sugar to taste – remember that half the charm of this traditional dish is its light, fruity freshness, so it should be quite tart. Stir in cinnamon if using, then beat until smooth with a wooden spoon. Turn into a dish and leave to become cold.

Whisk egg whites until they stand in shiny peaks. Lightly fold in the cold apple purée and spoon into individual glasses. Refrigerate. Immediately before serving, sprinkle with muscovado sugar and decorate with edible fresh flowers. Daisies look particularly lovely with this simple pudding. Eat with little dessert biscuits, homemade if possible.

Gooseberry Tansy

This very old pudding was so-called from the use of the herb tansy. It was chopped up with the fruit, but is seldom used in cookery today as it has rather a bitter flavour. Apples, rhubarb or plums can be used instead of gooseberries.

serves
4

450g (1lb) green gooseberries
115g (4oz) unsalted butter
2 egg yolks, beaten
150ml (¼ pint) double cream
about 2 tablespoons caster sugar
juice of ¼ lemon

Simmer gooseberries in the butter until cooked – about 15 minutes. Remove from heat and cool a little. Stir in beaten egg yolks and lightly whipped cream. Sweeten with sugar to taste. Bring to the boil very gently and, when thick, turn into a china serving bowl. Sprinkle with caster sugar and lemon juice. Serve cold.

Cranachan

A traditional Scottish pudding, which started life as a hot drink, similar to the Elizabethan version of syllabub, and was later thickened with oatmeal. Fragrant heather honey, Scotch whisky and Scottish raspberries are traditional, but other fruits and alcohol can be used.

serves 4–6

85g (3oz) coarse oatmeal
300ml (½ pint) double cream
50g (1¾oz) caster sugar
50ml (2fl oz) malt whisky
350g (12oz) fresh raspberries,
    reserving a few for decoration
sprigs of fresh mint

Sprinkle the oatmeal on to a baking tray. Bake in a preheated oven at 200°C (400°F, Gas mark 6), until browned and crisp, moving the oatmeal around to prevent sticking and burning. Remove from the oven and cool.

Whip the cream with the sugar and whisky, until it stands in fairly soft peaks. Gently fold in the cooled toasted oatmeal. Spoon into individual glasses, layering the raspberries between spoonfuls of the mixture, as you go. Serve decorated with a few raspberries and a sprig of fresh mint.

Cranachan with Strawberries

Quarter 600g (1lb 5oz) strawberries and leave to soak in 25g (1oz) caster sugar and 50ml (2fl oz) raspberry liqueur for at least 10 minutes. Gently heat the oatmeal and 50g (1¾oz) soft brown sugar for 2–3 minutes, stirring continuously until the sugar has dissolved and the oatmeal is golden and caramelized. Remove from the heat and spread the oatmeal on a plate to cool, breaking up any large clusters with a fork. Continue as before.

Whim-wham

This Edwardian trifle used Naples biscuits, the foundation for many 18th- and 19th-century desserts, instead of sponge cakes, and syllabub instead of custard. It is very rich, so serve small portions.

serves 6

300ml (½ pint) double cream
55g (2oz) caster sugar
2 tablespoons white wine
zest of 1 lemon
12 sponge finger or boudoir biscuits
225g (8oz) redcurrant, quince or apple jelly
25g (1oz) chopped candied orange peel

Put the cream, sugar, wine and lemon zest into a large bowl and whisk until thick to make the syllabub. Break the biscuits into several pieces and spoon layers of syllabub, biscuits and jelly alternately into an attractive glass bowl, ending with a layer of syllabub. Sprinkle with chopped candied orange peel and chill overnight.

Elderflower Trifle

Elderflowers were used widely in the past to flavour jellies, creams, flummeries, fools and trifles. Pick on a dry day. This trifle has a base of Amaretti or ratafia biscuits, with a syllabub topping. It looks prettiest in individual stemmed glasses.

**serves
4**

for the syllabub
zest and juice of 1 large lemon
1 large elderflower head in
    full bloom
125ml (4fl oz) white wine
85g (3oz) caster sugar
pinch of freshly grated nutmeg
300ml (½ pint) double cream
sprigs of elderflower to decorate

for the base
8 Amaretti biscuits
2 tablespoons homemade or
    good-quality elderflower cordial
2 tablespoons sweet sherry
2 tablespoons cold water

Begin by making the liquid base for the syllabub. Mix together the lemon zest, juice and flowers snipped from the elderflower head. Set aside to steep for at least 1 hour. Meanwhile, put the biscuits, broken, into 4 glasses. Mix the cordial, sherry and water together and pour equal amounts into each glass.

Strain the steeped syllabub liquid into a large bowl. Stir in the sugar and the nutmeg, then pour in the cream. Whisk together until the cream thickens, then spoon into the glasses.

Serve chilled and decorated with a few tiny sprigs of elderflower, either fresh or crystallized. Elderflower can be crystallized by dipping it into beaten egg white, then into sugar and leaving it on a wire rack to dry.

Damson Snow

This tasty dish also makes a super ice cream. Freeze in the normal way.

serves
6

900g (2lb) damsons
175g (6oz) caster sugar
90ml (3fl oz) cold water
425ml (¾ pint) double cream
2 tablespoons brandy or Marsala (optional)
3 egg whites

Put the washed and de-stalked damsons into a saucepan with sugar and water. Bring slowly to the boil and cook gently for 10–15 minutes or until the fruit is tender. Rub through a sieve and leave the damson pulp to get cold.

Lightly whip the cream with brandy or Marsala, if using, until thick. Whisk the egg whites until stiff and fold into cream mixture. Stir in the damson pulp reserving 1 tablespoon for decoration. Pour into individual glasses and chill well. Just before serving, stir in the reserved damson pulp to give a marbled effect, or just top with damson pulp. Serve with homemade dessert biscuits.

Edinburgh Fog
Omit the damsons. Whip the cream with 2 tablespoons sweet sherry or Madeira. Stir in 55g (2oz) ratafia biscuits and sweeten to taste with caster sugar. Chill well. Sprinkle generously with toasted flaked almonds and serve with fresh raspberries or strawberries.

Lemon Posset

A posset was an Elizabethan drink made of milk curdled with sack (sack is the old name of a Spanish wine rather like sherry) or claret, beer, ale and orange or lemon juice – rather like a syllabub. Breadcrumbs were added to thicken the posset so that it could be eaten rather than drunk. Later, these were omitted and beaten egg whites were used instead to make it lighter and not so rich.

600ml (1 pint) double or whipping cream
zest of 1½ lemons
150ml (¼ pint) dry white wine
4 tablespoons lemon juice
about 115g (4oz) caster sugar
3 large egg whites
2 tablespoons caster sugar
extra lemon zest for decorating

Beat the cream and lemon zest in a mixing bowl until thick. Beat in the wine until thick again. Add the lemon juice very gradually, beating all the time. Add sugar to taste and beat until stiff. Whisk the egg whites until stiff and standing in peaks, then whisk in the 2 tablespoons of sugar until smooth and glossy. Fold the egg whites into the cream mixture, then pile into a glass or china bowl. Serve chilled and decorated with lemon zest. Accompany with homemade dessert biscuits.

Orange Posset

Substitute the grated zest of 1 orange for 1 lemon and 2 tablespoons of orange juice for 2 tablespoons of the lemon juice. Decorate with orange zest.

Rhubarb & Orange Fool

Rhubarb was one of the last garden fruits to be cultivated for eating in Britain. It had been grown in China for its root, a powerful purgative, which was exported to Europe. In Tudor times the plants themselves were introduced into English herb gardens and medicinal rhubarb became a garden crop. The rhubarb we know now first arrived in the 17th century when John Parkinson received seeds from Italy which he planted in his garden. Its cultivation spread rapidly throughout Britain and it has remained one of the most popular garden fruits.

An old-fashioned rhubarb or spring fool is the perfect way to round off a spring dinner party, especially if the meal has been rather rich. Young forced rhubarb makes the best fool, because of its beautiful pink colour when cooked.

**serves
8–10**

900g (2lb) rhubarb
zest of 1 orange
½ teaspoon ground ginger
5cm (2in) stick cinnamon
25g (1oz) unsalted butter
about 175g (6oz) caster sugar

600ml (1 pint) double or
   whipping cream
2 tablespoons orange liqueur
   (optional)
primroses or other spring
   flowers to decorate

Cut the rhubarb into short lengths. Put in a large saucepan with the orange zest, ginger, cinnamon stick, butter and sugar. Cook over a gentle heat for about five minutes until the rhubarb is softened, thick and pulpy. Remove the cinnamon stick and cool completely.

Whip the cream with the liqueur, if using, until thick enough to hold its shape. Fold in the cold rhubarb pulp very lightly to give a marbled effect. Taste, and add more sugar if necessary. Spoon the fool into a deep glass bowl or individual glasses, and chill well before serving. Decorate with primroses, or other simple edible spring flowers.

Boodles Orange Fool

A speciality at Boodles Club in St James' Street, London, which was founded in 1762. It sounds simple, but is delicious. The idea of combining sponge with fruit fool dates back to the 18th-century version with ratafias.

serves 4–6

4 trifle sponges
zest and juice of 1 lemon
zest and juice of 2 oranges
55–85g (2–3oz) caster sugar
600ml (1 pint) double cream
crystallized orange peels or slices
crystallized angelica

Cut the sponge cakes into 1cm (½in) strips and line the base of a glass serving dish, or individual glass dishes. Mix the zest and juice of the citrus fruit with the sugar and stir until dissolved. Whip half the cream until thick but not stiff, and beat the juice into the cream slowly. Taste for sweetness. Spoon over the sponge cakes and chill thoroughly for 2–3 hours, until the juice has soaked into sponge and the cream has set. Whip the remaining cream until stiff, and pipe on top of the pudding to decorate. Decorate with crystallized fruit and angelica.

Gooseberry & Elderflower Fool

'Soft, pale, creamy, untroubled, the English fruit fool is the most frail and insubstantial of English summer dishes', wrote Elizabeth David. The fruit fool, probably named after the French verb *fouler*, meaning 'to crush', is one of the few quintessentially English puddings that should not be tampered with – for me, the perfect fool is just cream, fruit (flavoured or plain) and sugar.

Gooseberry fool has been very popular for centuries, but was particularly loved by the Victorians, who added egg-thickened custard. In this recipe I have gone back to basics, but flavoured the gooseberries with elderflowers, which are flowering at the same time. If you want to use frozen gooseberries out of season, elderflower cordial can be used instead, with less sugar. The fool mixture can be frozen as an ice cream.

serves 4–6

450g (1lb) green gooseberries
3 or 4 large elderflower heads
    in full bloom
1 tablespoon water
85–115g (3–4oz) caster sugar
300ml (½ pint) double cream

Wash and top and tail gooseberries. Put in a heavy saucepan with the elderflower heads tied together with cotton thread, the water and the sugar. Cook gently until the fruit is soft, then set aside to cool. Once cool, lift out the elderflower stalks – don't worry about leaving the flowers behind, they will add to the flavour.

Mash the gooseberries with a fork and taste for sweetness (if you prefer a smoother purée, rub the gooseberries through a plastic sieve). Leave to get completely cold.

Whip the double cream until thick and just beginning to hold its shape. Fold into gooseberry purée to give a swirled, marbled effect, then pile into a serving bowl or individual glasses. Decorate with small sprigs of elderflower, if in season. Serve with homemade biscuits.

Any fruits can be used to make fools, but for me, the most successful are berries, currants, apricots, the plum family and of course, rhubarb.

London Syllabub

Syllabub is one of the oldest known British dishes. London Syllabub is one example of a typical Georgian syllabub of the 'everlasting' type, which meant that it didn't separate into a honey-combed curd on the top with an alcoholic drink underneath. Allow the lemon or orange rind and rosemary to infuse in the fruit juice and the alcohol overnight if possible.

**serves
4–6**

finely pared rind of 1 lemon
    or 2 oranges
juice of 1 lemon or orange
sprig of fresh rosemary, bruised
150ml (¼ pint) white wine,
    dry sherry or Madeira

2 tablespoons brandy
85g (3oz) caster sugar or honey
300ml (½ pint) double cream
sprigs of fresh rosemary for
    decorating

Put the lemon or orange rind and juice and rosemary in a bowl with the wine and brandy and leave overnight. Next day, strain the wine and orange or lemon mixture into a saucepan. Add sugar or honey and heat gently until the sugar has dissolved. Pour into a large, deep bowl and leave to cool. Gradually stir in the cream, beating until it 'ribbons' and stands in soft peaks (don't use an electric blender or the cream may become grainy). Pour into individual glasses, or custard cups, and chill. Serve decorated with sprigs of rosemary. Also very good with Apple Fritters (see page 82).

Lavender Syllabub

Flavour with 2 sprigs of lavender, bruised well, instead of the rosemary. Serve decorated with lavender flowers. Many other herbs and flowers can be used to flavour syllabub. Lemon geranium leaves are also very successful. Use 8 bruised leaves to 300ml (½ pint) cream.

Spiced Syllabub

Infuse the rind of 1 orange, 1 lemon, 1 stick of cinnamon and 8 cloves in 200ml (7fl oz) decent red wine overnight, then continue as before. Serve decorated with orange zest.

Fine Orange Flummery

Flummery, a lovely pale slippery pudding related to syllabub and custard, is a delicious pure white jelly. In medieval times, cereals such as rice, oats or sago were cooked long and slowly with milk and flavourings. This was really the beginning of the flummery. In Tudor and Stuart times it became a much richer dish of cream flavoured with spices, orange-flower water, rose water, almonds or wine, set with calves' feet or isinglass. It was often coloured and eaten in the second course with cream or wine poured over.

Flummery is now easily set with gelatine and should be made in the most attractive mould you can find. It is still possible to pick up fairly cheaply elaborate Victorian china and glass jelly moulds in antique and junk shops. If possible, this dish should be made the day before you want to serve it.

serves 6

600ml (1 pint) double cream
50g (1¾oz) caster sugar
zest and juice of 2 oranges
1 tablespoon orange-flower water
3 tablespoons warm water
15g (½oz) gelatine

Put the cream, sugar, orange zest and juice and orange-flower water in a heavy saucepan and heat very gently until the sugar is completely dissolved and the cream is just coming to the boil. Leave on one side to cool.

Put warm water into a cup and sprinkle over gelatine. Stand the cup in a pan of water and heat gently, stirring, until the gelatine has dissolved. Pour through a warmed sieve into the cream mixture. Stir well. Pour into a mould and leave to cool. Refrigerate overnight. To turn out, dip the mould quickly in hot water. Serve chilled with a bowl of soft fruit and whipped cream.

Fine Orange & Madeira Flummery
Replace the orange-flower water with Madeira or sweet sherry.

Lemon Solid

This pudding's ancestor was the posset, but instead of being thickened with breadcrumbs, eggs and almond-flavoured biscuit crumbs, ground almonds were used. Lemon Solid is found in varying forms, in many old cookery books and is one of the glories of British cooking, despite its rather uninspiring name.

serves 6–8

600ml (1 pint) thick double cream
zest and juice of 2 lemons
115g (4oz) caster sugar
3–4 macaroons, homemade if possible

Put the cream, lemon zest and sugar in a saucepan. Stir over gentle heat for about 10 minutes until the sugar has completely dissolved, bringing just to the boil. Cool, stirring from time to time, and when almost cold add the strained lemon juice. Crumble the macaroons and put in the bottom of an attractive glass bowl. Pour the cold cream mixture over the macaroons. Chill overnight in the refrigerator. Serve chilled and decorated with lemon zest.

Little Chocolate Pots

serves
6

175g (6oz) good-quality plain chocolate
2 tablespoons water
15g (½oz) salted butter
3 eggs, separated

Break the chocolate into small pieces, then put in a basin with the water. Place over a pan of gently simmering water to melt the chocolate into a thick cream, stirring from time to time. Remove from the heat and stir in the butter. Beat in the egg yolks one at a time (they will be slightly cooked in the hot chocolate mixture). Leave to cool.

Whisk the egg whites until stiff, then briskly fold into the chocolate. When thoroughly mixed, pour into little custard pots or ramekins. Chill overnight. Serve with homemade dessert biscuits.

Little Chocolate & Orange Pots

Stir the zest of 1 large orange and 1 tablespoon orange liqueur into the melted chocolate with the butter.

Little Chocolate & Coffee Pots

Stir 1 tablespoon coffee essence or very strong espresso into the melted chocolate with the butter.

Iced Creams

Blackcurrant Ice Cream

This is an ice cream made using the custard method. Fresh or frozen berries, or homemade jam, sharpened with a squeeze of lemon – in which case omit the sugar – are successful. Any fruits can be used to make ice cream, but my favourites are damson, raspberry, a combination of rhubarb and redcurrant and blackberry as well as blackcurrant.

300ml (½ pint) double cream
300ml (½ pint) full-cream milk
4 eggs, separated
8 tablespoons caster sugar
450g (1lb) blackcurrants

Whisk the cream, milk, egg yolks and sugar together in a basin. Set over a pan of simmering water and continue whisking until the custard thickens enough to coat the spoon. Leave to cool.

Pick over the blackcurrants if using fresh fruit and remove any stalks. Liquidize the fruit to a thick purée and stir into the cooled custard.

Freeze the mixture until the edges are solid, but the middle is still soft – an hour or two. Beat the half-frozen mixture and fold in the egg whites, stiffly whisked. Freeze again until solid. Place in the refrigerator for 30 minutes before serving with thick cream.

Nesselrode Pudding

for the vanilla syrup
150ml (¼ pint) water
50g (1¾oz) granulated sugar
1 vanilla pod, split in half lengthways

for the ice cream
25g (1oz) candied peel, chopped
25g (1oz) raisins
25g (1oz) glacé cherries, quartered

25g (1oz) currants
2 egg yolks
50g (1¾oz) caster sugar
300ml (½ pint) single cream
225g (8oz) fresh or tinned
    unsweetened chestnut purée
1 tablespoon Maraschino liqueur
150ml (¼ pint) double or
    whipping cream

To make the vanilla syrup, bring the water, sugar and vanilla pod slowly to the bowl, stirring to dissolve the sugar. Boil rapidly for 5 minutes. Remove from heat and cool. When completely cold, remove the vanilla pod. (This can be washed and used again, so it is not as expensive as it might seem.)

Poach the candied peel, raisins, cherries and currants in the prepared vanilla syrup for a few minutes. Drain, reserving the syrup, and leave to cool.

Make a custard by beating the egg yolks with the sugar until thick and pale yellow in colour. Heat the single cream to simmering point in a heavy-based saucepan, and stir into the egg mixture. Strain back into the saucepan and stir continuously over gentle heat until the mixture thickens enough to coat the back of a spoon. Do not allow to boil. Pour into a large mixing bowl and leave to cool.

Mix the chestnut purée with reserved vanilla syrup and add to cooled custard with Maraschino. Stir well and pour into a lidded container. Freeze for 1 hour and then remove. Whip the cream until it stands in soft peaks and add to semi-set ice cream together with prepared raisins and currants. Freeze again until firm.

Serve topped with vanilla-flavoured cream and decorate with crystallized violets and angelica. This pudding looks very attractive frozen in a mould, turned out and then decorated with piped cream and grated chocolate or glacé cherries, crystallized violets or apricots – make it as decorative as you wish.

Elderflower Ice Cream

This creamy ice cream is very simple to make, particularly if you use a commercial elderflower cordial rather than making your own.

serves
4–6

egg whites from 2 large eggs
1 tablespoon caster sugar
300ml (½ pint) double cream

90ml (3fl oz) good-quality
   elderflower cordial
sprigs of elderflower, to decorate

Whisk the egg whites until stiff and beat in the sugar. Whip the cream until it stands in soft peaks, then beat in the elderflower cordial.

Fold the egg whites into the cream and turn the mixture into a lidded plastic container. Freeze for 4–5 hours until firm. Allow to soften in the refrigerator for 30 minutes before serving, scooped in stemmed glasses and decorated with elderflower, if in season.

Lemon Mint Ice Cream

serves
4–6

4 large eggs, separated
115g (4oz) caster sugar
300ml (½ pint) double cream

zest and juice of 2 large lemons
4 sprigs of strongly flavoured
   fresh mint

Whisk the egg whites until stiff, then whisk in the sugar, a little at a time, until the mixture is light and stands in peaks. Beat the egg yolks until pale, then fold into the egg white until thoroughly mixed. Whip the cream with the lemon zest and juice and add to the egg mixture. Chop the mint finely and fold into the mixture, then turn into a lidded plastic container and freeze as usual.

Vanilla Ice Cream

If you want a vanilla ice cream with real flavour, this recipe is for you, but leave the vanilla pod whole if you prefer a more neutral-base ice cream.

serves
6

1 vanilla pod
300ml (½½ pint) full-cream milk
3 large egg yolks
about 115g (4oz) caster sugar
300ml (½ pint) double cream

Split the vanilla pod lengthways then, using a small knife, strip out the seeds on to a white plate, so that you don't lose any. Put the seeds on one side for later. Put the milk and vanilla pod (without the seeds) into a saucepan. Bring slowly to the boil, stirring occasionally. Draw off the heat, cover and leave for 20 minutes to infuse.

Whisk the egg yolks in a bowl with the sugar and vanilla seeds, then whisk in the vanilla-infused milk, including the pod. Set the bowl over a pan of gently simmering water and cook, stirring continuously, until the custard thickens and covers the back of a wooden spoon. Taste and add more sugar if you wish. Leave to cool, then strain.

Whip the cream lightly and fold into the custard, then pour into a lidded plastic container and freeze as usual. Half an hour before serving, transfer to the refrigerator to soften, before serving – divine with Rich Chocolate Pudding (see page 188).

Vanilla & Walnut Ice Cream

The addition of toasted walnuts to the above recipe makes a stunning ice cream. Spread 85g (3oz) chopped walnuts on to a baking tray and toast in a preheated oven at 200°C (400°F, Gas mark 6) for 4–7 minutes, shaking them once or twice. Tip into a metal sieve and shake to dislodge flakes of papery skin, which should be discarded. Leave to cool. When your ice cream is semi-frozen, fold in the toasted walnuts. Return to the freezer to set solid.

Marmalade Ripple

Any marmalade may be used in this recipe depending on your personal taste, but top-quality thick-cut Seville is too strong except for the most dedicated marmalade lovers.

4 large eggs, separated
1 tablespoon lemon juice
115g (4oz) caster sugar
425ml (¾ pint) double or
    whipping cream
4–8 tablespoons marmalade (to taste)
1 tablespoon orange liqueur

Beat the egg yolks with the lemon juice and caster sugar until pale and frothy. Whip the cream until it stands in soft peaks and add to the egg mixture. Whisk the egg whites until soft and fold gently into the mixture. Pour into a lidded plastic container and freeze. When the mixture is almost frozen, mix together the marmalade and orange liqueur, then fold into the ice cream to create a gorgeous ripple effect.

Honey & Brandy Ice Cream

serves 6–8

4 large eggs, separated
115g (4oz) caster sugar
4 tablespoons clear honey, warmed
425ml (¾ pint) double cream
6 tablespoons brandy or cider brandy

Beat the egg yolks and sugar until pale in colour. Add the warmed honey a little at a time, beating continuously, until pale and fluffy, then put to one side. Whisk the cream with the brandy until it forms soft peaks. Whisk the egg whites in a separate bowl, until stiff. Pour the egg-yolk mixture into a large bowl, then fold in a quarter of the cream, followed by a quarter of the egg white. Repeat until all the cream and egg whites have been incorporated into the yolk mixture. Pour into a lidded plastic container and freeze in the usual way.

This recipe makes a softer ice cream than usual because of the alcohol content, so it can be served straight from the freezer. Scoop into bowls or glasses and serve with Butterscotch or Coffee Sauce (see pages 203 and 209), or with a little poached seasonal fruit, such as rhubarb, gooseberries or plums.

Stem Ginger Ice Cream

This is a delicious ice cream and ideal for serving at Christmas lunch as an alternative to Christmas pud or as a refreshing alternative to brandy butter. It is very good served with meringues flavoured with ground ginger.

serves 6–8

4 eggs, separated
115g (4oz) caster sugar
1 teaspoon ground ginger
2 tablespoons brandy

425ml (¾ pint) double or
whipping cream
6 large pieces stem ginger
in syrup, chopped

Beat the egg yolks with the sugar, ground ginger and brandy. Whip the cream until it stands in soft peaks and add to the egg mixture. Whisk the egg whites until stiff and fold into the mixture. Pour into a lidded container and freeze for about 1 hour. Add 4 of the pieces of chopped stem ginger and stir evenly into semi-set ice cream. Return to freezer until completely set.

Scoop into glasses, sprinkle with the remaining chopped ginger and pour over a little of the stem ginger syrup. Top with Easy Chocolate Sauce (see page 202) or Butterscotch Sauce (see page 203).

Chestnut & Chocolate Ice Cream

Years ago, chestnuts were grown and used in cooking much more than they are today. You will find this ice cream very delicate and unusual in flavour. Use fresh or tinned unsweetened chestnut purée. You can melt 85g (3oz) good-quality plain chocolate and add to the ice cream after the first stage of freezing, if preferred.

serves 6–8

4 eggs, separated
115g (4oz) caster or soft brown sugar
2–3 drops vanilla essence
225g (8oz) unsweetened
    chestnut purée

450ml (16fl oz) double or
    whipping cream
marrons glacés to decorate
    (optional)

Beat the egg yolks with the sugar and vanilla essence. Stir in the chestnut purée. Whip cream until it stands in soft peaks and add to the chestnut mixture. Whisk the egg whites until stiff and fold gently into the mixture. Pour into a lidded container and freeze for about 1½ hours until mushy.

Remove the ice cream from the freezer and stir gently. Replace in the freezer and leave to freeze completely. Take the ice cream out of freezer 30 minutes before you want to serve it, and leave in the refrigerator to soften and improve in flavour. Scoop into stemmed glasses and top with Easy Chocolate Sauce (see page 202) and marrons glacés, if desired. Particularly good at Christmas.

Ratafia Ice Cream

serves 6–8

115g (4oz) ratafia biscuits
150ml (¼ pint) sweet sherry
4 eggs, separated
85g (3oz) caster sugar
425ml (½ pint) double or whipping cream
25g (1oz) chopped toasted almonds

Crush the ratafia biscuits and soak in sherry for 20 minutes. Beat the egg yolks and sugar until thick and pale yellow in colour. Whip the cream until it stands in peaks and add to the egg mixture. Fold in the soaked ratafia biscuits. Whisk the egg whites until stiff and fold into the mixture. Freeze in a lidded container for about 1 hour and then beat mixture and add the chopped toasted almonds. Replace in the freezer and leave to set completely.

About 30 minutes before serving, move from the freezer into the refrigerator and leave to soften. Serve topped with Eliza Acton's Madeira Sauce (see page 211) or with seasonal soft fruit and cream.

Fried Puddings

Apple Fritters

serves
6

115g (4oz) plain flour
pinch of salt
½ teaspoon ground cinnamon
150ml (¼ pint) tepid water
2 tablespoons orange liqueur
1 tablespoon vegetable oil
4 medium cooking or crisp
   dessert apples
zest and juice of ½ lemon

50g (1¾oz) icing sugar
25g (1oz) caster sugar
6 tablespoons apricot jam or thick
   orange marmalade
2 tablespoons water
fat for deep frying (lard or oil)
2 egg whites
caster sugar for dredging
orange or lemon segments, for serving

Sieve the flour, salt and cinnamon together into a basin. Make a well in the centre. Gradually blend in the tepid water and 1 tablespoon liqueur, followed by the oil. Beat vigorously with a rotary hand or electric whisk to make a smooth, glossy batter. Cover and leave to stand in a cool place for at least 30 minutes, to allow the starch grains in the flour to absorb water and swell.

Peel, core and slice the apples in 6mm (¼in) thick slices. Mix together the lemon zest and juice, 1 tablespoon liqueur and sieved icing sugar. Add the apple slices and coat evenly. In a heavy saucepan dissolve caster sugar and jam over a low heat. Dilute with water to make a syrup of coating consistency. Simmer the syrup for 1 minute and keep warm. Coat each soaked apple ring in this syrup, allowing excess to drain off. Leave apple rings on one side to dry out a little.

When ready to cook the fritters, heat fat for deep frying – when a blue vapour rises from the fat, it is hot enough. Test by dropping in a little batter, which will rise if the fat is the correct temperature; if not, the batter will sink. Make sure your fat is absolutely clean and at least 7.5cm (3in) deep. Whisk egg whites until very stiff and fold into prepared batter. Using cooking tongs or a long skewer, dip the apple rings, one at a time, into batter, allowing excess to drain off. Lower carefully into hot fat and deep-fry until crisp and puffed, turning them over once or twice. Avoid frying too many at once, because this cools the fat and does not allow room for fritters to expand properly. When cooked, remove from fat and drain on crumpled kitchen paper. Serve immediately, dredged with caster sugar and thick cream or with Orange and Lemon Sauce (see page 213).

Traditional Lemon Pancakes

Although probably not of British origin, pancakes have been established here for so many centuries that they may be considered a national institution. When Lent was strictly observed, eggs and fatty foods were forbidden for forty days and so pancake-making became associated with Shrove Tuesday in the UK, to use up any remaining eggs, butter and milk before the fasting.

<table>
<tr><td>makes
10</td><td>115g (4oz) plain flour
pinch of salt
zest of 1 lemon
1 egg
300ml (½ pint) milk
15g (½oz) melted butter, plus
    extra for frying
caster sugar, for sprinkling
2 lemons, for serving</td></tr>
</table>

Sieve flour and salt together into a basin. Stir in the lemon zest. Make a well in the centre and break in the egg. Beat well, incorporating the flour, and add half the milk very gradually, beating all the time until a smooth batter is formed. Add the remaining milk a little at a time and beat until well mixed. Leave to stand for at least 30 minutes.

Stir the melted butter into the batter just before cooking. Heat a very little butter in a pancake or omelet pan until very hot. Spoon in a tablespoon of batter and tip the pan until the batter covers its base. Cook until golden brown underneath. Turn over with a palette knife and cook the other side until golden. Turn out on to sugared greaseproof paper, sprinkle with caster sugar and a squeeze of lemon juice. Serve immediately with extra sugar and lemon wedges, or keep warm in the oven until you are ready to serve up.

Sweet Apple Omelet

The ancestor of the British omelet, known as a 'herbolace', was a mixture of eggs and shredded herbs baked in a buttered dish. Cheese and milk were added later. This herbolace was replaced by the French 'omelette' in the 14th century, referred to in many English recipes as an 'aumelette' or 'alumelle', which gradually became omelet.

serves 4

2 large cooking apples
115g (4oz) butter
115g (4oz) caster sugar
2 tablespoons apple brandy or rum

150ml (¼ pint) double
or whipping cream
5 eggs
pinch of salt

Peel, core and slice the apples. Fry the apples gently in 50g (1¾oz) butter, turning frequently until tender. Remove from heat and stir with 50g (1¾oz) caster sugar, apple brandy and double or whipping cream.

Separate 2 of the eggs and beat the egg yolks and 3 whole eggs together – keep the whites. Add salt and 25g (1oz) caster sugar. Whisk the 2 egg whites until stiff and gently fold into the egg mixture.

In a frying pan, melt the remaining butter. When light brown in colour, pour in the egg mixture and cook over a moderate heat, mixing it well with a fork to allow the uncooked egg to run on to the bottom of the hot pan. Cook until golden brown on the bottom and cooked on the top (sweet omelets, unlike savoury omelets, should not be runny on the top). Spread the apple mixture over the top, fold in half and slide on to a warmed plate. Sprinkle with the remaining caster sugar and caramelize by placing the omelet under a very hot grill for a few minutes.

Another attractive way of finishing this omelet is to heat a skewer until it is red hot and then very carefully draw it over the top of the sugar-sprinkled omelet in a criss-cross pattern.

Puffed Strawberry Omelet

A fluffy sweet omelet flavoured with orange zest and orange-flower water and filled with fresh strawberries. This kind of omelet was known as a popular treat over a hundred years ago.

serves
2

3 eggs, separated
2 level teaspoons caster sugar
zest of 1 orange
½ teaspoon orange-flower water
    (optional)
2 tablespoons water

15g (½oz) butter
225g (8oz) sliced strawberries
25g (1oz) icing sugar, sifted
1 tablespoon Grand Marnier
    (optional)

Whisk the egg whites with the caster sugar until stiff, but not dry. Beat the egg yolks, orange zest, orange-flower water, if using, and water until creamy. Melt the butter in an omelet or small frying pan over a low heat. Fold the egg whites carefully into yolks using a metal spoon. Be careful not to overmix. Tip the omelet pan to coat sides with butter. Pour in the egg mixture. Cook the egg mixture over a moderate heat until golden brown underneath and just firm to touch in the centre. Place under a pre-heated grill and cook until just set. Spread with sliced strawberries and sprinkle with sifted icing sugar. Fold the omelet and slide gently on to a hot serving plate. Dredge with more icing sugar. Warm the Grand Marnier, if using, in a small saucepan, pour over the omelet and set alight. Take to table immediately while the omelet is still flaming. Serve with sweetened whipped cream.

Puffed Lemon Omelet

Replace 1 tablespoon of the water with lemon juice, and use lemon zest instead of orange. Omit the orange-flower water and add a little more caster sugar. Serve without the strawberry filling. Set alight with brandy if you like.

New College Puddings

Traditionally served at New College, Oxford, in the 19th century, these puddings first appeared in a recipe book by Dr William Kitchiner published in 1831. They were basically suet puddings which were fried instead of boiled, reducing the cooking time considerably.

serves
6

115g (4oz) suet
115g (4oz) fresh white breadcrumbs
50g (1¾oz) caster or soft brown sugar
15g (½oz) baking powder
pinch of salt
½ teaspoon grated nutmeg

zest of 1 orange
115g (4oz) currants
25g (1oz) candied peel
3 eggs, separated
2 tablespoons brandy (optional)
butter, for frying

Mix the suet, breadcrumbs, sugar, baking powder, salt and nutmeg with the orange zest, currants and candied peel, stirring thoroughly. Beat the egg yolks and mix with brandy, if using. Stir into the pudding mixture. Whisk the egg whites and gently fold into the pudding mix, which should be a soft consistency that drops easily.

Melt some butter in a heavy frying pan and fry tablespoonfuls of pudding mixture in hot butter, flattening the mixture as you cook it (like a fish cake). Turn once, frying each side for about 6 minutes until brown. Serve hot, sprinkled with sugar, and with Vanilla Custard Sauce (see page 207).

Poor Knights of Windsor

A traditional pudding from Berkshire – where the alleged poverty of medieval knights was jokingly commemorated – consisting of bread, soaked in sherry or wine, eggs and cream, and fried. It is an excellent way of using up leftover bread or rolls.

serves
6

6 thick slices of white bread
2 eggs
2 teaspoons caster sugar
150ml (¼ pint) single cream
   or milk
pinch of ground cinnamon
zest of ½ lemon

2 tablespoons Madeira or
   sweet sherry
butter and oil for frying
extra caster sugar and cinnamon,
   for sprinkling
orange or lemon wedges,
   for serving

Remove the crusts from the bread and cut each slice into 3 fingers. Beat the eggs and sugar together in a basin. Heat the cream or milk until it just reaches boiling point. Cool a little before pouring on to egg mixture, beating continuously. Stir in cinnamon, lemon zest and Madeira or sherry.

Melt a little butter and oil in a heavy frying pan. Dip each finger or piece of bread into the custard mixture and fry until golden brown and crisp. Drain on crumpled kitchen paper and keep warm until all the bread has been fried. Sprinkle with a little caster sugar and ground cinnamon. Serve with orange or lemon wedges.

Eggy Bread with Maple Fried Apples

Melt 15g (½oz) butter in a frying pan and add 2 crisp dessert apples, unpeeled, cored and thickly sliced, 1 tablespoon pure maple syrup and a generous pinch of ground cinnamon. Cook over medium heat for about 10 minutes until the apples are just tender. Cook the pudding as above, then serve the fingers of fried bread topped with the apples and pan juices. Serve with thick cream if you wish.

Quire of Paper

Much admired by 17th- and 18th-century cooks, a quire of paper consisted of a pile of wafer-thin pancakes. The batter, rich with eggs and cream, was run as thinly as possible over the bottom of a heavy pan and cooked on one side only. The completed pancakes were dredged with caster sugar and laid evenly one upon another until the pile contained twenty. A wine sauce and melted butter were served with the pancakes, which were cut into wedges like a cake.

This recipe will make a pile of about ten thin pancakes, but if you use a smaller 18cm (7in) pan you can make more. The pancakes can be spread individually with jam, jelly or fruit purée and cream.

serves 6

115g (4oz) plain flour
pinch of salt
25g (1oz) caster sugar
2 eggs
2 egg yolks

300ml (½½ pint) single cream
2 tablespoons medium sherry
   or Madeira
unsalted butter for frying
caster sugar, for sprinkling

Sieve the flour and the salt together into a basin. Stir in the sugar. Make a well in the centre of the flour. Put the eggs and egg yolks into the well and gradually mix the eggs and flour together. Add the cream gradually, beating well until a smooth batter is formed. Stir in the sherry or Madeira to make a thin cream.

Heat a heavy-based pancake or omelet pan, brush with melted butter and add 1 tablespoon of batter. Twist the pan until the bottom is evenly coated with batter and cook until the pancake is golden brown on the bottom. Remove from the pan or turn over and cook the other side. Keep warm in a clean tea towel.

Make a stack of pancakes, filling them with jam and whipped cream or whatever you choose. Sprinkle liberally with caster sugar. Serve hot, cut in wedges with Eliza Acton's Madeira Sauce (see page 211).

Fruit & Jellies

Black Caps

Apples were first baked in the ashes of the fire. The skins were often burnt on one side, hence the name Black Caps. Baked apples, frequently cooked in cider or wine, have continued to be a country favourite for centuries. They can be filled with any dried fruit and are delicious topped with honey, jam or marmalade.

The secret of a good baked apple is to use a quality cooking apple, preferably a Bramley, which is Britain's finest cooking apple. It was first grown in Nottinghamshire by an innkeeper and butcher called Matthew Bramley from Southwell, and introduced commercially in 1876. The Bramley is one of the late croppers and is large with a shiny green skin. It is very crisp and cooks superbly.

serves 6

6 large Bramley cooking apples
50g (1¾oz) chopped dates
50g (1¾oz) sultanas
50g (1¾oz) raisins
25g (1oz) chopped almonds
 or hazelnuts
zest and juice of 1 orange

85g (3oz) soft brown sugar
1 level teaspoon ground mace
 or mixed spice
40g (1½oz) butter
150ml (¼ pint) sweet sherry
 or Madeira

Wash and core the apples. Score the skin around the middle of each apple to prevent it bursting during baking, and stand close together in a well-buttered ovenproof dish. Mix the chopped dates, sultanas, raisins and chopped nuts with the orange zest and juice. Pack the centres of apples with this mixture. Mix the brown sugar and spice together and sprinkle over each apple. Top with a knob of butter.

Pour sherry or Madeira around the apples and bake in the centre of a preheated oven at 180°C (350°F, Gas mark 4) for 45–60 minutes, basting occasionally. Serve warm, topped with thick cream and Honey and Brandy Ice Cream (see page 74) or Stem Ginger Ice Cream (see page 75) and extra brown sugar.

Spiced Pears in Red Wine

serves
4

4 large, good-shaped hard pears
   with stalks
300ml (½ pint) red wine
85g (3oz) caster sugar
1 vanilla pod, split in half lengthways

1 small cinnamon stick
4 cloves
zest of 1 orange
1 thick slice of fresh ginger, peeled
1 rounded teaspoon arrowroot

Preheat the oven to 120°C (250°F, Gas mark ½). Peel the pears thinly, leaving the stalks intact, and cut a thin slice from the bottom of each pear so that they stand upright easily. Lay the pears on their side in a flameproof casserole dish with a tight-fitting lid.

Pour over the wine and sprinkle over the sugar. Scrape the seeds out of the vanilla pod and add to the casserole with the pod, cinnamon stick, cloves, orange zest and ginger.

Bring everything up to simmering point, then cover the casserole and bake on a low shelf in the oven for about 1½ hours. Now turn the pears on to their other side and cook for a further 1½ hours. When the pears are cooked, carefully lift them out with a slotted spoon, standing them upright in a dish.

Strain the cooking liquor into a bowl, then pour back into the casserole. Place over direct heat. Mix the arrowroot to a smooth paste with a little cold water, then add to the wine mixture, whisking all the time. Bring just up to simmering point when the liquor will have thickened. Remove from the heat and cool.

Spoon over the pears when cool and baste well. Cover the dish with foil and chill thoroughly in the refrigerator, basting frequently, with the wine sauce. Serve bathed in the sauce, with thick cream.

Pears in Nightshirts

serves
6

6 large firm dessert pears
425ml (¾pint) cider
700g (1lb 9oz) cooking apples
15g (½oz) butter
zest of 1 lemon
1 tablespoon lemon juice
2–3 cloves

85g–115g (3–4oz) caster sugar
85g (3oz) icing sugar, sifted
6 egg whites
pinch of salt
350g (12oz) caster sugar
50g (1oz) toasted
    flaked almonds

Peel the pears, but leave on the stalks. Put the cider into a saucepan large enough to take the pears. Bring to the boil and lower the pears gently into this liquor using a slotted spoon. Cover and simmer very gently for 30–35 minutes or until the pears are translucent and just tender.

While the pears are cooking, make the apple pulp. Peel, core and slice the apples. Rub butter over the sides and the bottom of a saucepan. Add the apple slices, lemon zest, lemon juice and cloves. Cover with buttered greaseproof paper and cook over a low heat for about 15 minutes until the apples are soft and any liquid has evaporated. Stir gently from time to time. Remove the cloves and beat the apples to a smooth, thick pulp with a wooden spoon. Add sugar to taste. Pour into a buttered ovenproof dish large enough to take the pears, allowing room for the meringue coating.

Drain the cooked pears and roll each one in sifted icing sugar. Place the pears on top of apple pulp. Whisk the egg whites until very stiff. Add 175g (6oz) caster sugar and whisk until stiff and glossy. Fold in the remaining 175g (6oz) caster sugar and spread or pipe a thick coating of meringue over the pears. Bake in a preheated oven at 200°C (400°F, Gas mark 6) for 10–15 minutes or until the meringue is crisp and light brown. Serve immediately, sprinkled with toasted flaked almonds.

Brandied Peaches

Peaches were introduced by the Romans and by the 17th century there were 22 varieties growing in Britain. Recipes for brandied fruit, one of the early ways of preserving, began to appear at the beginning of the 18th century. Peaches, nectarines, apricots, cherries and grapes were packed into earthenware jars containing brandy and a little sugar syrup. The jars were sealed closely and the fruit was ready for future use.

serves 6

6 fresh peaches
juice of 1 lemon
12 cloves
300ml (½ pint) cold water
115g (4oz) granulated sugar

5cm (2in) piece of
    cinnamon stick
1 bay leaf
25g (1oz) butter
2 tablespoons brandy

Cover the peaches with boiling water for about 2 minutes. Remove from the water, and skin. Halve and stone the peaches. Brush all over with lemon juice to stop them discolouring. Stick a clove in each half. Put the water, sugar, cinnamon stick, bay leaf and butter into a small saucepan. Bring slowly to the boil to dissolve the sugar. When it has completely dissolved, boil for 5 minutes to make a sugar syrup. Place the peaches in a shallow ovenproof dish. Add brandy to the sugar syrup and pour over the peaches. Cover and bake in the centre of a preheated oven at 160°C (325°F, Gas mark 3) for about 30 minutes, or until the peaches are tender, but still hold their shape. Remove the bay leaf and cinnamon stick and serve either hot or cold with whipped cream.

Nectarines in Baked Cream

This delicious fruit has been known in Britain since the early 17th century and was frequently grown in the walled gardens of great houses. Peaches, pears and apricots are equally good in this simple but tasty recipe.

serves
6

6 fresh nectarines
300ml (½ pint) double cream
115g (4oz) caster sugar
1 vanilla pod, split in half lengthways
25g (1oz) toasted flaked almonds

Skin the nectarines by dropping in boiling water for a few minutes. Remove the stones by running a knife round the fruit and twisting the two halves in opposite directions. Place the nectarine halves in a shallow ovenproof dish. Heat the cream, sugar and vanilla pod together gently until the sugar has dissolved. Pour the cream over nectarines (don't remove the vanilla pod). Bake in the centre of a moderate oven at 180°C (350°F, Gas mark 4) for 30–40 minutes or until the fruit is tender. Remove from the oven and chill well.

Serve very cold, sprinkled with toasted flaked almonds. This dish is also very good served with hot Easy Chocolate Sauce (see page 202) dribbled generously over the cream.

Creamy Nectarine Tart

Line a 30cm (12in) flan tin with shortcrust pastry. Bake blind for 10–15 minutes at 200°C (400°F, Gas mark 6) – see Apricot Amber Pudding on page 32 for instructions on baking blind. Fill the cooked pastry case with the nectarine mixture as above and bake for a further 30 minutes.

Baked Quinces in Cinnamon Syrup

Quinces have been grown in Britain since Anglo-Saxon times, when they were probably eaten stewed with honey. The first marmalade to arrive here in medieval days from southern Europe was made from the fruit (*marmelo* is Portuguese for 'quince') and in Elizabethan times the fruit was particularly highly regarded. So we have had a long love affair with the quince – and hurray, it is back in fashion. If you have room in your garden, plant an old-fashioned quince tree – it is a thing of beauty all year round.

The quince needs long, slow cooking to turn its dry, pale yellow flesh into an extraordinary deep pinky-red succulent delight, but it's well worth the effort. The sweet, musky perfume given off is indescribable and the flavour is delicious.

serves
4

6 quinces
juice of 2 lemons
1 vanilla pod, split in half
    lengthways

200g (7oz) caster sugar
about 300ml (½ pint) water
1 small stick of cinnamon
4 cloves

Peel 4 of the quinces and cut into quarters. Remove the cores and place in a large, heavy lidded ovenproof dish, arranging the fruit in a single layer. Pour over the lemon juice to prevent discolouration.

Use the remaining 2 quinces to make the syrup. Peel, core and chop them coarsely, then place in a pan with the vanilla pod seeds and half the sugar. Add enough water to cover. Bring to the boil and simmer for about 1 hour, or until the quinces are very soft and the liquid has turned syrupy. Strain and discard the quince pulp.

Pour the syrup over the prepared quince quarters, adding the cinnamon, cloves and remaining sugar. Make sure the quinces are covered by the syrup, adding a little more water, if necessary. Place a piece of greaseproof paper on top to keep the fruit submerged. Cover with the lid of the pan and place in a preheated oven at 120°C (250°F, Gas mark ½) and cook for 2–3 hours, or until the quinces are soft to touch and golden in colour. Serve warm with Vanilla Custard Sauce (see page 207), Honey and Brandy Ice Cream (see page 74) or with thick cream.

Rhubarb & Red Wine Jelly

An ideal, elegant pudding, after a rich meal. Use young, pink, forced, rhubarb for the best colour and flavour.

serves 6–8

450g (1lb) young or forced rhubarb
5cm (2in) piece of fresh ginger
150g (5½oz) cane sugar
juice of 2 lemons

juice of 2 oranges
850ml (1½ pints) red wine
4 tablespoons water
40g (1½oz) gelatine

Cut the rhubarb into 2.5cm (1in) pieces and place in a large pan with the peeled and roughly chopped ginger. Add the sugar and strain the lemon and orange juices into the mixture through a fine sieve, then add the wine.

Set the pan over the heat, bring to the boil, then simmer gently for about 15 minutes, or until the rhubarb is completely mushy. Remove the pan from the heat and strain the liquid through the finest sieve into another bowl or a clean pan. Don't press the rhubarb against the sieve, or the juices will become cloudy.

Put the 4 tablespoons of water into a small pan, bring to bubbling point and remove from the heat. Sprinkle over the gelatine and stir until completely dissolved. Pass through a sieve into the rhubarb and wine liquor, then pour into a 1.3 litre (2¼ pint) jelly mould. Leave until cold, then transfer to the refrigerator to set.

Just before serving, dip the mould in hot water for a few seconds, then turn the jelly out on to a cake stand or serving plate, giving it a good shake to release it. Decorate with primroses, or other edible spring flowers and serve with cream.

Clare College Mush

Also called Eton Mess, the original recipe for this traditional pudding is said to have come from Clare College, Cambridge. A delicious combination of strawberries, cream and crushed meringues, it can be flavoured with an orange or berry liqueur or vanilla. Other fruits work well – raspberries, and poached apricots, rhubarb, damsons and plums are favourites, but best of all I like a combination of strawberries and raspberries with a flavouring of liqueur and half cream and half yoghurt.

serves
6

2 large egg whites
55g (2oz) caster sugar
55g (2oz) icing sugar
225g (8oz) fresh strawberries
225g (8oz) fresh raspberries

1 tablespoon (plus an extra dash)
   raspberry liqueur
200ml (7fl oz) double cream
200ml (7fl oz) natural yoghurt

Preheat the oven to 110°C (225°F, Gas mark ¼). Whisk the egg whites until they form soft peaks, then beat in the caster sugar a little at a time. Continue whisking for a further 10 minutes until the mix is smooth and shiny, then sift in the icing sugar. Spoon on to non-stick baking paper arranged on a baking tray, then bake in the oven until dry, but with a slightly soft, chewy centre – about 2 hours. Remove from the oven and leave to cool on a wire rack.

When ready to assemble the pudding – and it is best eaten within 2 hours of making – cut the strawberries into halves or quarters, depending on their size, then toss with a dash of raspberry liqueur. Stir in the raspberries, reserving a few of the best for decoration.

Lightly whip the cream and yoghurt with a tablespoon of raspberry liqueur. Break the meringues into walnut-sized pieces and gently stir into the cream mixture with the fruit (don't overmix, because it looks very attractive with a raspberry-ripple effect).

Spoon the mixture into glass dishes and serve chilled, decorated with the reserved raspberries.

Summer Pudding

The true old-fashioned Summer Pudding was made with raspberries and redcurrants only, but if you wish, you can include small halved strawberries, white currants, blueberries, sweet, firm-fleshed cherries and a few blackcurrants – not too many of the latter or they will dominate the pudding. If you are lucky enough to be able to get hold of some mulberries, they make a delicious summer pudding, combined with half the amount of strawberries. Make sure you use good-quality bread.

serves 6

700g (1lb 9oz) fresh raspberries
200g (7oz) fresh redcurrants
115g (4oz) vanilla caster sugar or plain
    caster sugar
about 6 slices of day-old white bread
    about 8mm (⅜in) thick
2 tablespoons raspberry liqueur

Put the fruit into a heavy saucepan and sprinkle over the sugar. Heat gently for 3–4 minutes only, until the sugar has dissolved and the juices have begun to flow. Cut the crusts off the bread and use it to line an 850ml–1.2l (1½–2 pint) pudding basin, bottom and sides. Overlap the slices slightly so that there are no gaps. Spoon the fruit into the basin, reserving a little of the juice for serving. Pour the raspberry liqueur over the fruit before finishing with a top layer of bread.

Put a plate on top that fits exactly inside the basin and weight it fairly heavily. Leave the pudding in the refrigerator overnight. Turn out just before serving and pour the reserved juice over any bread that isn't quite soaked through. Serve chilled with pouring cream or softly whipped double cream.

Cherries in Red Wine

serves 6

900g (2lb) dark red cherries
25g (1oz) sugar
pinch of ground cinnamon
150ml (¼ pint) red wine
3 tablespoons redcurrant jelly
juice of 1 orange

1–1½ dessertspoons arrowroot
1–2 tablespoons cold water
3–4 sugar lumps
1 orange
300ml (½ pint) double cream

Stone the cherries and place in a saucepan with the sugar and cinnamon. Cover the pan and heat gently until the juices run freely – about 7–10 minutes. By this time the cherries will be at boiling point. Remove from heat, drain the cherries and turn into a serving bowl, reserving the juice.

Put the wine in the saucepan and boil rapidly until reduced by half. Add the redcurrant jelly and orange juice and heat gently until the jelly has melted. Add the juice from the cherries. Dissolve 1 dessertspoon of arrowroot in 1 tablespoon of water and add this to the saucepan. Bring to boiling point again. The liquor should now be smooth and rich looking but not gluey. Pour juice over cherries and chill.

Rub sugar lumps over the rind of the orange until they are orange-coloured and well impregnated. Crush them in a bowl and add the strained juice of the orange. Whip the cream lightly, until it will barely hold its shape. Fold in the orange syrup. Chill well.

Serve the orange cream separately or pour over the top of the cherries in their serving bowl. Decorate with orange zest and whole cherries.

Moonshine

This romantically named pudding is a lemony jelly, popular with 17th- and 18th-century cooks. Saffron would probably have been used to colour the jelly in the 17th century as highly coloured foods were extremely popular. Make it in a fancy Victorian mould if you have one.

serves
4–6

115g (4oz) caster sugar
finely pared rind of 2 lemons
600ml (1 pint) cold water
juice of 2 lemons, strained
15g (½oz) gelatine

Put the sugar, lemon rind and water in a saucepan. Bring to the boil and simmer for 15 minutes to allow the lemon rind to infuse. Leave on one side to cool. Strain. Put the strained lemon juice in a cup and sprinkle over gelatine. Place the cup in a pan of water and gently heat until the gelatine has melted, strain through a warmed fine-mesh sieve into the cooled lemon syrup. Stir well to make sure the gelatine is mixed in thoroughly. Leave to cool again and, when just beginning to set, whisk until the jelly looks like snow. Turn into a wetted mould and refrigerate until set.

Turn out on to an attractive plate by dipping the mould quickly in hot water. Serve chilled and decorated with a few small edible flowers and maidenhair fern, if you have a plant. Eat with homemade dessert biscuits.

Plums in Sloe Gin

Large Victoria plums have the best flavour for this dish, so make the most of them when they are in season.

serves
4–6

900g (2lb) firm, but ripe, plums
115g (4oz) soft brown sugar
1 teaspoon vanilla extract
200ml (7fl oz) sloe gin, homemade
    or bought

Preheat the oven to 180°C (350°F, Gas mark 4). Halve and stone the plums, then place them in one layer in a large shallow ovenproof dish. Sprinkle with the sugar.

Stir the vanilla extract into the sloe gin and pour over the plums. Cover tightly with foil and place in the oven for about 45 minutes. Baste the plums once during this time, taking care not to break them up. The plums should be cooked, but not falling apart and sitting in a puddle of gloriously boozy crimson syrup.

Serve the plums barely warm, or at room temperature, with their juices and some thick cream.

Figs Baked in Wine

In the past, figs have been much more popular in British cookery than they are now. They were ripened in sheltered gardens in the south of England. There is something rather luxurious about fresh figs for pudding.

**serves
4–6**

40g (1½oz) butter, at room
    temperature
12 fresh ripe figs
1½ teaspoons vanilla extract

115g (4oz) demerara sugar,
    or 4 tablespoons clear honey
100ml (3½fl oz) white wine
50ml (2fl oz) Marsala

Preheat the oven to 180°C (350°F, Gas mark 4). Smear the butter on a shallow ovenproof dish, large enough to hold all the figs snugly together. Wash and dry the figs, then cut a deep cross in the top, without cutting through them completely. Arrange them in the dish, sprinkle with vanilla extract and sugar, then pour the wine and Marsala around the figs.

Cover with foil and put on a high shelf in the oven for 20 minutes, then uncover and cook for a further 20 minutes. Serve 2 figs per person with thick cream or Vanilla Ice Cream (see page 71) and the syrup drizzled around the dish.

Port Wine Jelly

This posh jelly makes a very good alternative to plum pudding for Christmas lunch.

serves
6

300ml (½ pint) cold water
115g (4oz) cane sugar, preferably cube
1 tablespoon redcurrant jelly
2.5cm (1in) piece of cinnamon stick
3 cloves
1 bay leaf

zest of 1 lemon
1 blade of mace
300ml (½ pint) ruby port
1 tablespoon brandy
15g (½oz) gelatine

Place the cold water, sugar, redcurrant jelly, cinnamon stick, cloves, bay leaf, lemon zest and mace in a clean saucepan over gentle heat, stirring occasionally. When the sugar has completely dissolved and the jelly has melted, bring to the boil. Simmer for 10 minutes.

Put the port and brandy into a second clean saucepan and heat gently. Sprinkle on the gelatine and bring to the boil. Simmer for 10 minutes. Strain the contents of both saucepans through a fine sieve into a large jug, stir, and as the jelly cools pour into 6 stemmed glass dishes. Leave to set in the refrigerator. Serve chilled with pouring cream and homemade shortbread.

Milk Puddings, Custards & Trifles

Old-fashioned Rice Pudding

In Georgian times a rice pudding could be a very elaborate dish. It was either tied loosely in a cloth, boiled and eaten with melted butter, sugar or salt, or a richer dish including eggs, cream, butter, marrow, currants, brandy, ratafia, nutmeg and candied peel was baked with 'a paste round the edge'. You can flavour your pudding with lemon or orange zest, ground cinnamon or nutmeg, ½ vanilla pod (split lengthways), a few drops of rose water, a few saffron threads or 1 fresh bay leaf. The important thing is to cook the rice very slowly if it is to achieve that unctuous richness and a buttery brown crust. If you have an Aga or similar stove, leave it in the lowest oven overnight, though you will need to add more milk.

serves 4–6.

55g (2oz) short-grain rice
850ml (1½ pints) full-cream milk
25g (1oz) butter, cut into
    little pieces
pinch of salt

55g (2oz) caster sugar or 1 level
    tablespoon clear honey
1 curl of lemon rind
150ml (¼ pint) double cream
freshly grated nutmeg

Put the rice, milk, butter, salt, sugar or honey and lemon rind into a buttered ovenproof dish. Stir well, then add the cream. Stir again, then grate over plenty of nutmeg. Place uncovered in a preheated slow oven at 140°C (275°F, Gas mark 1) and cook for 3–4 hours, or until just starting to set. As the pudding cools, it will finish cooking in its own heat and thicken. Remove from the oven and leave until just warm, or cold, if you like.

Rice Pudding Meringue

Make a meringue topping with 2 egg whites and 115g (4oz) caster sugar. Pile on top of the rice pudding and return to the oven to brown the meringue.

Rice Creams

This delicate creamy pudding can be served with fresh soft fruit or any fruit sauce. It is basically a cold rice pudding, mixed with cream, but this description doesn't do it justice.

serves
4–6

55g (2oz) short-grain rice
300ml (½ pint) full-cream milk
25g (1oz) caster sugar
1 vanilla pod
1 bay leaf
1 level teaspoon gelatine
2 eggs, separated
300ml (½ pint) double or whipping cream

Wash the rice in cold water, drain and put in a heavy saucepan with the milk, sugar, vanilla pod and bay leaf. Bring slowly to the boil, then cook over gentle heat, stirring now and again to stop rice sticking on the bottom of the pan, until tender – about 40–45 minutes.

Remove from the heat and take out the vanilla pod and bay leaf. Sprinkle the gelatine into the hot rice and stir until dissolved. Beat the egg yolks with 1 tablespoon cream and stir into the rice. Return the pan to the heat for a few minutes, and then place in a bowl of cold water. Stir until cool, but not set.

Whip the remainder of the cream, until it begins to ribbon but does not stand in peaks. Whisk the egg whites until very stiff. Fold the cream into the cool rice, followed by the egg whites. Pour into individual glasses and chill before serving. Decorate with a few raspberries or strawberries and place the glasses on saucers covered with a fern leaf or strawberry leaves.

Spicy Ground Rice Pudding

This recipe is based on one by Eliza Acton, one of the best known of the 19th-century cookery writers. Eggs are added to make a richer pudding. Pies and puddings were often 'iced' or topped with egg whites as in this recipe.

serves
4–6

40g (1½oz) ground rice or semolina
600ml (1 pint) full-cream milk
strip of lemon peel
1 vanilla pod
1 bay leaf
pinch of ground nutmeg
25g (1oz) caster sugar or
    ½ tablespoon honey

2 eggs, separated
25g (1oz) butter
grated nutmeg or ground cinnamon
    for sprinkling
115g (4oz) caster sugar

Butter thoroughly a 1.2 litre (2 pint) ovenproof dish. Mix the ground rice or semolina to a smooth paste with a little of the milk in a basin. Boil the rest of the milk with the lemon peel, vanilla pod, bay leaf and pinch of nutmeg. Pour on to the ground rice or semolina, stirring continuously. Rinse the pan in which the milk was boiled and leave a film of cold water on the bottom. Return the rice and milk and bring slowly to the boil again, stirring all the time, so that it does not burn on the bottom of the saucepan. Cook gently for 10 minutes. Add the sugar or honey. Beat the egg yolks and beat into the rice. Remove the vanilla pod, bay leaf and lemon peel. Pour into the prepared pie dish. Dot with butter and sprinkle with nutmeg or cinnamon.

Bake in the centre of a preheated oven at 180°C (350°F, Gas mark 4) for about 25 minutes. Meanwhile, whisk egg whites until stiff and whisk in 50g (1¾oz) caster sugar. Fold in the remaining caster sugar. Pile the sweetened egg whites on top of the pudding and bake for a further 20 minutes until the meringue is crisp and lightly browned. Serve hot with pouring cream and a fruit sauce.

Durham Fluffin'

A milk pudding traditionally eaten in the north-east of England on Christmas Eve. The pearl barley has to be soaked in water overnight.

serves
6

2 tablespoons pearl barley, soaked overnight in water
600ml (1 pint) full-cream milk
¾ teaspoon grated nutmeg
a few drops of brandy
50g (1¾oz) soft brown sugar or 1 tablespoon honey
crystallized orange slices for decorating

Simmer the soaked pearl barley in the milk for about 30 minutes or until it is a smooth cream. Add grated nutmeg, brandy, and sugar or honey to taste. Serve hot in individual dishes with plenty of pouring cream, decorated with crystallized orange slices or with cream and Jam Sauce (see page 210).

Queen's Pudding

Also called Queen of Puddings, this dish was named after Queen Victoria and was created by her chefs at Buckingham Palace, but it was, in fact, based on a much older 17th-century recipe – a milk pudding thickened with breadcrumbs and eggs. It was originally baked in a 'puff paste' case. Try using lemon or lime curd instead of jam.

serves
6

85g (3oz) fresh white breadcrumbs
3 eggs, separated
200g (7oz) caster sugar
600ml (1 pint) full-cream milk

25g (1oz) butter
zest of ½ lemon
3 tablespoons raspberry jam

Butter a 1.2 litre (2 pint) ovenproof dish. Sprinkle the breadcrumbs in the bottom of the dish. Beat the egg yolks with 25g (1oz) caster sugar. Put the milk, butter and lemon zest into a saucepan and bring slowly to the boil. Leave to cool a little and then pour on to the egg yolks, stirring continuously until the mixture is smooth. Strain the custard over the breadcrumbs and leave to soak for at least 15 minutes. Stand the dish in a roasting tin half-filled with hot water and bake in the centre of a preheated oven at 180°C (350°F, Gas mark 4) for 25–30 minutes, or until lightly set. Warm the jam and spread over the top of the pudding. Whisk the egg whites until very stiff and add 85g (3oz) caster sugar. Whisk again until stiff and glossy. Fold in remaining sugar. Pile or pipe the meringue on top of the jam. Sprinkle with extra sugar and bake for a further 15–20 minutes or until the meringue is crisp and lightly browned.

Serve warm, with or without Jam Sauce (see page 210) and pouring cream, or cold with fresh raspberries and cream.

Manchester Pudding

Put a layer of apricot jam in the bottom of an ovenproof dish. Continue as before, but include 2 tablespoons of sherry or brandy in the custard. When the pudding is lightly set, spread with more apricot jam, and top with meringue as before. Serve warm or cold with pouring cream and poached fresh apricots.

Caramel Pudding

This is a very elegant pudding which appeals to even the most jaded of appetites. The custard pudding is covered with a beautiful caramel sauce, and is delicious served with fresh strawberries or raspberries. Try flavouring with orange zest and juice instead of brandy.

serves 6

115g (4oz) lump sugar
4 tablespoons cold water
1 teaspoon boiling water
600ml (1 pint) full-cream milk
1 vanilla pod

1 bay leaf
2 eggs
3 egg yolks
2 tablespoons caster sugar
1 tablespoon brandy (optional)

Preheat the oven to 160°C (325°F, Gas mark 3). Warm a 15cm (6in) souffle dish, or a 15cm (6in) cake tin or a fluted mould (this makes a very attractive pudding) in the oven. You can also use individual moulds.

Put the sugar and cold water in a heavy-based saucepan. Heat gently until the sugar has dissolved. Bring to the boil and boil rapidly without stirring until a rich brown caramel is formed. Remove from heat, add boiling water and pour into the warmed dish or mould. Using oven gloves or a tea towel, tip the mould carefully to coat the bottom and sides with hot caramel. Leave to get cold.

Heat the milk with the vanilla pod and bay leaf. Leave to stand for 30 minutes to infuse. Bring to the boil and remove the vanilla pod and bay leaf. Beat the eggs, egg yolks and sugar together until pale in colour. Pour the cooled milk on to the egg mixture a little at a time to avoid curdling the eggs, stirring continuously. Stir in brandy, if using. Strain the custard into the prepared mould. Stand in a roasting tin half-filled with hot water and bake in the centre of a preheated oven for about 45 minutes (30 minutes for individual moulds) or until the custard is set. Cooking time will vary depending on the mould you have chosen.

When cooked, remove the pudding from the oven, leave to cool completely and refrigerate before unmoulding. To unmould, loosen the edges of the pudding with the point of a knife. Place a shallow serving dish over the mould and turn out quickly. Serve chilled with soft fruit.

Queen Mab's Pudding

This pudding is based on a recipe by Eliza Acton, from her *Modern Cookery*, published in 1845. It is really a custard, set with gelatine, with candied fruits added to make it richer. Candying was a method of preserving fruit, popular in Tudor and Stuart days. Whole fruits were candied and served at the banquet course after the main meal, as well as being chopped and used in cakes, puddings and biscuits. If possible buy whole candied peel and chop it yourself.

serves 4–6

600ml (1 pint) full-cream milk
1 bay leaf
1 vanilla pod
strip of lemon peel
2 large eggs, separated
40g (1½oz) caster sugar

2 tablespoons warm water
15g (½oz) gelatine
50g (1¾oz) chopped glacé cherries
25g (1oz) chopped candied citron or
  lemon peel

Put the milk, bay leaf, vanilla pod and lemon peel in a saucepan and bring slowly to the boil. Remove from the heat and cool a little. Beat the egg yolks and sugar together and pour on the flavoured milk, stirring continuously. Remove the bay leaf, vanilla pod and lemon peel. Rinse the milk pan with cold water, leaving a film of water on the bottom, and return the milk and egg mixture to the pan. Heat gently, stirring all the time and cook until thick enough to coat the back of a wooden spoon. Remove from heat.

Put warm water in a cup and sprinkle over gelatine. Place the cup in a pan of water and heat gently until the gelatine has dissolved. Pour through a warmed fine-mesh sieve into the custard. Whisk the egg whites very stiffly and fold into cooled custard. Pour into a wetted mould and leave in a cool place until almost set. Stir in chopped cherries and peel and refrigerate to set completely.

Serve with a fruit sauce poured around the pudding.

Butter'd Oranges

Custard made with butter and eggs was a popular pudding during the 17th and 18th centuries. This recipe is more like an orange cheese or curd rather than a custard. It is very rich but also delightfully refreshing.

serves 6

thinly pared rind of 2 oranges
juice of 1 orange
1 tablespoon concentrated orange juice
50g (1¾oz) caster sugar
4 egg yolks

3 egg whites
225g (8oz) unsalted butter
1 large piece candied orange peel
150ml (¼ pint) whipping cream
slices of fresh orange

Put the orange rind in a small saucepan of boiling water and boil for 20 minutes or until soft. Drain and purée the rind in a blender or pass through a food mill or just pound orange rind with a rolling pin. Add the orange juices and sugar to the peel and beat until the sugar has dissolved. Add the egg yolks and egg whites and whisk until mixture is thick and smooth. Melt the butter and leave until cool, but not beginning to harden. Pour the butter in a steady stream into the egg and orange mixture and blend in a liquidizer for about 3 minutes, or beat with a rotary whisk for about 10 minutes. Refrigerate, beating occasionally until thick and beginning to set. Cut candied orange rind into tiny pieces, or shred with a grater. Fold into half-set orange custard. Pour into individual glasses or custard pots and chill well. Decorate, before serving, with whipped cream and orange slices.

Floating Islands

This Georgian pudding consists of a rich custard covered with poached meringues (the islands).

serves
6–8

600ml (1 pint) single cream
6 egg yolks
2 level teaspoons cornflour
175g (6oz) caster sugar
1 tablespoon rose water
850ml (1½ pints) milk, for poaching

1 vanilla pod
4 egg whites
pinch of salt
crystallized rose petals
toasted flaked almonds

Bring the cream gently to the boil in a heavy saucepan. Remove from heat and cool a little. Cream the egg yolks, cornflour and 50g (1¾oz) sugar until almost white. Pour the hot cream over the egg-yolk mixture gradually, beating all the time. Rinse out the saucepan, leaving a film of cold water on the bottom. Return custard to the saucepan and heat gently, stirring continuously until thick enough to coat the back of a wooden spoon (don't boil or the mixture will curdle). Remove from the heat and cool a little before stirring in rose water. Strain into a shallow serving bowl, sprinkle with sugar and leave to cool.

To make the 'islands', fill a frying pan with milk, flavoured with a vanilla pod, and bring to simmering point. Whisk the egg whites with a pinch of salt until they stand in stiff peaks. Whisk in 115g (4oz) caster sugar gradually, until smooth and shiny. Remove the vanilla pod from the pan. Using a tablespoon rinsed in cold water between each addition, spoon 4 islands into the pan of simmering water. Poach on each side for 2–3 minutes, until firm. Remove each island and drain on a clean towel. Repeat until the meringue mixture is used up (about 8 islands). Leave to cool. Arrange the islands on the 'lake' of custard and chill. To serve, sprinkle with crushed crystallized rose petals and toasted flaked almonds.

Trinity Burnt Cream

Also known as Cambridge Cream or Trinity Pudding, this pudding was first introduced to Trinity College, Cambridge by a Fellow in 1879 and served at dinner during May Week. It was brought in on a large silver dish and the caramelized top was cracked with great ceremony.

The recipe is said to have been based on an ancient Scottish dish which may have been brought over from France by Mary, Queen of Scots. It is similar to the delicious French crème brulée. There are endless versions of this creamy pudding with different flavourings – lemon zest, vanilla pod, or a bay leaf. The sugary top used to be browned by a 'salamander', a flat iron which was heated and passed over the top of the pudding. You can make this custard in one large baking dish or individual ovenproof dishes, and it is best made the day before you want to serve.

serves 4–6

600ml (1 pint) double cream
1 vanilla pod split lengthways
5 egg yolks
1 tablespoon caster sugar
about 4 tablespoons demerara sugar

Bring the cream with the vanilla pod very gently to the boil, in a saucepan. Leave to cool a little, then remove the vanilla pod. Cream the egg yolks and sugar together in a basin until almost white. Pour the hot cream on to the yolks in a steady stream, whisking all the time. Strain into a shallow 700ml (1¼ pint) ovenproof dish and place in a roasting tin filled with enough hot water to come halfway up the sides of the dish. Cook in a preheated oven at 150°C (300°F, Gas mark 2) for 1–1¼ hours or until just set.

Remove the dish from the oven and leave until cold. Chill in the refrigerator overnight, if possible. Just before serving, spread the demerara sugar in an even layer over the surface of the custard and spray with a little water (this helps caramelize). Heat a grill to its highest temperature, then place the pudding as near to the grill as possible until the sugar has melted and caramelized (if you have a chef's blowtorch, use this instead). Return the pudding to the refrigerator for 30 minutes before serving. Decorate with a few edible flowers (optional) and accompanied by a bowl of fresh cherries, strawberries or raspberries in season.

Devonshire Junket

This was a junket covered with clotted cream, popular in Devon and Cornwall – so simple, but so delicious. Junket has been made since the 13th century and is probably of Norman origin. Its name comes from the word *jonquette*, French for the little rush baskets in which it was made. The original junket was a rich confection of cream, curdled with rennet and flavoured with spices. Later, rose water and orange-flower water were added and junket was eaten alongside the jellies and flummeries at the end of a meal. It was traditionally served in beautiful junket bowls with stewed fruit, but is especially good with fresh raspberries or strawberries.

serves 4

600ml (1 pint) Jersey milk
   or single cream
1 heaped tablespoon caster sugar
1 tablespoon brandy

pinch of freshly grated nutmeg,
   plus extra for sprinkling
1 level teaspoon rennet
clotted cream, to serve

Heat the milk or cream to 38°C (100°F). Stir in the sugar to dissolve it, followed by the brandy, nutmeg and rennet. Stir well, then pour into a glass bowl or 4 individual serving dishes and leave to set at room temperature (not in the refrigerator), for about 4 hours.

Chill in the refrigerator for about 1 hour before serving plain or sprinkled with grated nutmeg and accompanied by clotted cream and soft fruit or purée of raspberries or strawberries.

Damask Cream

For a junket popular in 18th-century Bath, make the junket using single cream rather than milk and omitting the brandy. Sprinkle with grated nutmeg. About 30 minutes before serving, mix together 4 tablespoons double or whipping cream, 3 tablespoons rose water and 1 tablespoon caster sugar. Pour this over the top of the junket. Serve with pink or red rose petals strewn over the top. Alternatively, mix 4 tablespoons clotted cream with the rose water and sugar and serve separately with the junket.

Rich Cabinet Pudding
with Orange Sauce

serves
6

1 tablespoon brandy
1 teaspoon orange zest
1 teaspoon candied orange peel
a little unsalted butter
a few natural glacé cherries,
    halved
a little crystallized angelica
2 trifle sponges
25g (1oz) ratafia biscuits
600ml (1 pint) single cream

1 vanilla pod, split in half lengthways
6 eggs
1 tablespoon caster sugar
1 teaspoon cornflour

for the orange sauce
150ml (¼ pint) fresh orange juice
caster sugar to taste
a little potato flour or arrowroot
½ teaspoon orange zest

Soak the orange zest and candied peel in the brandy. Grease a soufflé dish with the unsalted butter and line the bottom with buttered greaseproof paper. Decorate the bottom with glacé cherry halves and crystallized angelica. Cut the sponges into small squares and arrange over the candied fruit, with the ratafias crumbled on top.

Bring the cream and vanilla pod to the boil very slowly, then cool a little. Cream the eggs, sugar and cornflour together in a basin, then strain the cream on to the egg mixture, stirring vigorously. Add the soaked orange zest, peel and brandy to the custard, then pour carefully over the cake in the mould. Leave to soak for about 15 minutes, then cover tightly with foil and tie down with string. Steam gently for about 1 hour or until the custard is set and firm.

Meanwhile, make the sauce. Bring the orange juice and sugar to the boil. Mix a little potato flour or arrowroot in a tablespoon of cold water, stir this into the boiling juice a little at a time until you have the required consistency. Add the orange zest. Dredge with caster sugar to prevent a skin forming. Serve the pudding hot with a little orange sauce.

Fine Almond Blancmange

Although its actual name is undoubtedly of French origin, blancmange has been known in Britain for many centuries. It is mentioned in some of the oldest cookery books as 'blewe manger' or 'blank mange' or 'white food'. Chaucer, in *The Canterbury Tales*, describes it as a mixture of 'minced capon with flour, cream and sugar'. In fact, it was made with any white meat stewed with rice, dried fruits, almonds and spices. Exactly when the meat was omitted is not known, but by Elizabethan times the dish had become a mixture of cream, sugar and rose water, thickened with egg yolks.

The English blancmange of the 18th century was a kind of jelly, stiffened with isinglass or hartshorn and flavoured with almonds and rose water. By the early 1820s, arrowroot was being exported to Britain from the West Indies and became the thickening agent. Boiling milk, sweetened and seasoned with cinnamon, mace, and lemon peel, was poured on to a solution of arrowroot. It was set in elaborate moulds – and here was the true forerunner of our modern cornflour blancmange.

serves
4–6

40g (1½oz) cornflour
300ml (½ pint) milk
300ml (½ pint) single cream
1 bay leaf

strip of lemon peel
2 tablespoons caster sugar
4–5 drops almond essence
25g (1oz) toasted flaked almonds

Mix the cornflour to a smooth paste with a little of the milk. Heat the rest of the milk and cream in a saucepan with the bay leaf and lemon peel and gradually blend in the cornflour mixture. Bring to simmering point and cook for about 3 minutes, stirring continuously until thickened. Remove from the heat and sweeten to taste. Stir in almond essence. Pour into a fancy 600ml (1 pint) mould, rinsed out with cold water. Put in the refrigerator to set. Unmould on to a plate, decorate with toasted almonds and serve with fresh soft fruit or a fruit sauce and pouring cream or yoghurt.

Try experimenting with different flavourings like chocolate, coffee, lemon, orange, brandy or other liqueurs, and vanilla.

Mrs Beeton's Gooseberry Trifle

In this recipe, gooseberry pulp has replaced the more usual sponge cake at the bottom of the trifle, and is covered with a rich custard and topped with a 'whip', which was a Victorian version of syllabub. If possible, make the syllabub topping a day in advance. Any fruit pulp can be used.

serves
6

zest and juice of 1 lemon
6 tablespoons sweet white wine
   or sherry
2 tablespoons brandy
50g (1¾oz) caster sugar
600ml (1 pint) double cream

700g (1lb 9oz) green gooseberries
3 tablespoons cold water
250g (9oz) caster sugar
strip of lemon rind
4 egg yolks
1 level teaspoon cornflour

Put lemon zest and juice into a small bowl. Stir in wine or sherry, brandy and sugar until the sugar has dissolved. Cover and leave for several hours to infuse. Strain the liquid into a clean bowl and stir in 300ml (½ pint) of the cream gradually, beating until it almost reaches a soft-peak stage (don't use an electric beater. If overbeaten, syllabub will become grainy). Chill overnight.

Next day, top and tail the gooseberries and put in a heavy saucepan with the water and 50g (1¾oz) sugar. Simmer gently for about 20 minutes until soft. Rub through a sieve or beat to a pulp. Add 175g (6oz) sugar – you may need more, if the gooseberries are tart. Put in a shallow serving bowl and leave to cool.

Bring the remaining 300ml (½ pint) of cream slowly to the boil with the strip of lemon rind, and leave on one side to cool a little. Cream the egg yolks, cornflour and 25g (1oz) caster sugar together until almost white. Remove the lemon rind and pour on the hot cream in a steady stream, beating all the time. Rinse out the saucepan used for heating the cream, leaving a film of water in the bottom. Return the egg mixture to the pan and heat gently until thick enough to coat the back of a wooden spoon (don't boil because the custard will curdle). Remove from heat and leave to cool. Pour over the gooseberry pulp. Sprinkle with caster sugar to stop a skin forming and leave to get completely cold.

Pile prepared syllabub on top of the custard and chill well. Just before serving, decorate with twists of lemon rind or lemon slices and sprigs of fresh rosemary.

Old-English Sherry Trifle

for the base
1 fatless sponge cake made with
   3 eggs, 85g (3oz) caster sugar
   and 85g (3oz) plain flour or
   1 packet of trifle sponges
good-quality apricot jam or apple
   or quince jelly
115g (4oz) ratafia biscuits or
   macaroons
about 6 tablespoons medium
   sherry or Madeira
2 tablespoons brandy (optional)

for the custard
600ml (1 pint) single or
   double cream
1 vanilla pod, split in half
   lengthways
50g (1¾oz) caster sugar
2 teaspoons cornflour
6 egg yolks

for the topping
425ml (¾ pint) double or
   whipping cream

Cut the sponge into 2.5cm (1in) slices and liberally spread with chosen preserve. Arrange in a large glass bowl. Scatter over the ratafia biscuits or macaroons, then sprinkle liberally with sherry or Madeira and brandy, if using.

To make the custard, bring the cream with the vanilla pod to the boil. Mix the sugar with cornflour, add the egg yolks gradually and beat well until smooth. Remove vanilla pod from the milk and pour on to the egg mixture, stirring all the time. Rinse out the milk pan, leaving a film of cold water in the bottom. Return the custard to the pan and stir well with a wooden spoon over a low heat until thick. Immediately the custard is thick enough, plunge the bottom of the pan into a bowl of cold water to stop the mixture curdling. Leave to cool a little.

When the custard is fairly cool, pour over the sponge, and leave to cool completely. When cool, whip the cream until it stands in peaks and spread a thick layer over the custard. Pipe the top with the remaining cream and decorate with lots of crystallized fruits, nuts and extra ratafias – the more the merrier, especially at Christmas. In the summer, the trifle looks lovely decorated with crystallized flowers, rose petals or fresh edible flowers.

Apple & Brandy Trifle

serves
6–8

for the base
1 fatless sponge made with
    3 eggs, 85g (3oz) caster sugar,
    85g (3oz) plain flour
    or 1 packet trifle sponges
about 6 tablespoons apple brandy

for the apple layer
3 large Bramley apples
3 Cox's apples
2 tablespoons light soft brown sugar
½ teaspoon ground cinnamon

for the custard
425ml (¾ pint) double cream

1 vanilla pod, split in half
    lengthways
2 large eggs
egg yolks from 2 large eggs
85g (3oz) caster sugar

for the cream topping
300ml (½ pint) double cream
25g (1oz) icing sugar
vanilla extract to taste

for decoration
100g (3½oz) flaked almonds
25g (1oz) icing sugar
3 tablespoons apple brandy

Cut the sponge into 2.5cm (1in) slices and arrange in a large bowl. Pour over the apple brandy and leave for at least 30 minutes to soak in. To make the apple layer, peel, core and roughly chop the apples. Place in a saucepan with the sugar and cinnamon. Cook over a medium heat until the apples are tender; leave to cool.

To make the custard, pour the double cream into a saucepan with the vanilla pod and bring to the boil. Meanwhile, mix the eggs, egg yolks and sugar together in a large bowl. When the cream reaches boiling point, pour it over the egg mixture, whisking continuously to prevent the eggs from curdling. Strain through a fine sieve into a large bowl. Place over a pan of simmering water. Heat until the custard has thickened, whisking from time to time. Set aside to cool. Cover the soaked sponge with a layer of the apple mixture, then a layer of custard.

For the cream topping, whisk together the cream, icing sugar and vanilla until it forms soft peaks. Spoon on top of the custard. Mix the almonds, icing sugar and apple brandy together in a small bowl. Tip out on to a baking tray and toast in a preheated oven at 180°C (350°F, Gas mark 4) for 15 minutes, or until golden brown. Leave to cool, then scatter over the cream.

Pies,
Tarts & Flans

Lemon Meringue Pie

for the pastry
175g (6oz) plain flour
1 tablespoon icing sugar
115g (4oz) cold butter, cut in
  small pieces
1 egg yolk
about 1 tablespoon ice-cold water

for the filling
115g (4oz) caster sugar
2 level tablespoons cornflour

zest of 2 large lemons
125ml (4fl oz) lemon juice
juice of 1 small orange
85g (3oz) butter, cut in small pieces
3 egg yolks
1 whole egg

for the meringue
4 egg whites, at room temperature
225g (8oz) caster sugar
2 level teaspoons cornflour

To make the pastry, sieve the flour and icing sugar together into a mixing bowl. Lightly rub in the butter, then add the egg yolk and enough water to mix to a dough. Knead briefly into a smooth ball, then roll out and line a buttered 23cm (9in) loose-bottomed, fluted flan tin. Prick the base with a fork, line with foil and chill for 30 minutes to 1 hour or overnight. Put a baking sheet in the oven and preheat to 200°C (400°F, Gas mark 6). Bake blind in the usual way (see Apricot Amber Pudding, page 32). Remove from the oven and set aside. Lower the oven to 180°C (350°F, Gas mark 4).

To make the filling, mix the sugar, cornflour and lemon zest in a medium saucepan. Strain and stir in the lemon juice gradually. Make the orange juice up to 200ml (7fl oz) with water and strain into the pan. Cook over a medium heat, stirring continuously, until thick and smooth. Once the mixture bubbles, remove from the heat and beat in the butter until melted. Beat the egg yolks and whole egg together, then add to the pan and return to the heat. Keep stirring vigorously for a few minutes until the mixture thickens and plops from the spoon. Remove from the heat and set aside.

Whisk the egg whites to soft peaks, then add half the sugar, a spoonful at a time, whisking between each addition without overbeating. Whisk in the cornflour, then add the rest of the sugar as before until smooth and glossy. Quickly reheat the filling and pour it into the pastry case. Immediately pile spoonfuls of meringue around the edge of the filling (if you start in the middle, the meringue may sink), then spread so it just touches the pastry (to anchor it and help stop it sliding). Pile the remaining meringue into the centre, spreading so that it touches the surface of the hot filling and starts to cook, then give it all a swirl. Return to the oven for 18–20 minutes until the meringue is crisp.

Remove from the oven and leave in the tin for 30 minutes, then remove and leave for at least another 30 minutes to 1 hour before serving. Eat the same day, or the meringue will be spoiled.

Seville Orange Tart

Oranges began to arrive in England at the end of the 13th century from southern Europe, but were extremely expensive and always of the bitter Seville type. It wasn't until the 16th century that sweet oranges were first brought back from Ceylon by the Portuguese.

Use Seville oranges when in season for this recipe, or sharpen sweet oranges with the juice of a lemon.

serves
6

175g (6oz) sweet shortcrust pastry
    (see Chocolate and Prune Tart
    page 158, but add zest of ½ lemon)

for the filling
zest and juice of 2 Seville oranges
55g (2oz) caster sugar
55g (2oz) cake crumbs (Madeira-type)
25g (1oz) butter, cut into small pieces
150ml (¼ pint) single cream or
    full-cream milk
2 eggs, separated

Roll out the pastry and use to line a 23cm (9in) flan ring. Chill, then bake blind (see Apricot Amber Pudding, page 32). Reduce the oven to 180°C (350°F, Gas mark 4).

Mix the orange zest with the sugar until it turns yellowy-orange, then add the cake crumbs and the butter. Warm the cream or milk and pour over the mixture. Stir until the butter has melted, then stir in the egg yolks and the orange juice. Whisk the egg whites until they stand in soft peaks, then fold in gently. Spoon the mixture into the pastry case and bake for 30 minutes until set and golden brown. Serve warm or cold with cream.

Taffety Tart

serves
4–6

for the pastry
175g (6oz) plain flour
50g (1¾oz) semolina
2 tablespoons icing sugar
pinch of salt
zest and juice of 1 orange
115g (4oz) butter

for the filling
1 large orange
2 large eggs
115g (4oz) caster sugar
1 large Bramley apple,
    peeled and grated

To make the pastry, sieve the flour, semolina, icing sugar and salt together into a mixing bowl. Gently heat the orange zest, juice and butter in a small pan until bubbling. Remove from the heat and leave to cool for a few minutes. Gradually stir into the flour mixture to make a dough. Roll out and use to line a buttered 20cm (8in) flan tin. Chill well for 30 minutes, then bake blind in the usual way (see Apricot Amber Pudding, page 32).

To make the filling, grate the rind of the orange, then remove the segments taking off the pith and reserving as much juice as possible. Beat the eggs and sugar together well and add the orange segments, rind, juice and grated apple. Pour into the cooled pastry case and bake in a preheated oven at 180°C (350°F, Gas mark 4) for about 30 minutes until the top is golden.

Serve warm with Vanilla Custard Sauce (see page 207) or Creamy Marmalade Sauce (see page 212) or Marmalade Ripple ice cream (see page 72) or with cream. Also very good cold with cream.

Apple & Cheesecrust Pie

Apple pies were flavoured with candied orange peel, saffron, cloves, cinnamon and dates until the 18th century, when lemon zest and juice was favoured and this combination has continued to be popular. Wild fruits like blackberries, bilberries and elderberries were added by the poor, to make the apples and the pie go further. The traditional combination of apple and cheese has inspired the use of cheese pastry in this recipe.

serves
6

for the pastry
175g (6oz) plain flour
115g (4oz) butter, cut in
    small pieces
115g (4oz) Cheddar cheese,
    finely grated
1 egg yolk
about 1 tablespoon
    ice-cold water

for the filling
700g (1lb 9oz) Bramley apples
225g (8oz) Cox's apples
50g (1¾oz) butter
about 85g (3oz) soft brown sugar
pinch of ground cinnamon
zest of ½ lemon
50g (1¾oz) raisins (optional)
juice of 1 lemon
a little milk and caster sugar, to glaze

To make the cheese pastry, sieve the flour into a mixing bowl, then rub in the butter. Stir in the grated cheese, then mix to a dough with the egg yolk and water. Knead lightly, then chill in the refrigerator.

Cut each apple into thick slices and fry gently in the butter, sprinkling with sugar. Add the cinnamon and lemon zest, then place in a shallow, buttered 23cm (9in) pie dish with the raisins, if using. Pour over the lemon juice and leave to cool.

Roll out the chilled pastry and use to make a lid for the pie. Make a hole in the centre, brush with milk and then sprinkle lightly with caster sugar. Bake in a preheated oven at 190°C (375°F, Gas mark 5) for 20–30 minutes, or until the pastry is golden brown.

Apple Pasties

A pasty refers to any sweet and savoury ingredients folded and enclosed in pastry. It is the pride of the West Country, especially Cornwall. Originally the pasty was invented for the men to take to work to keep them going through the long working day. Any flavourings and spices can be added, and try using different combinations of fruit.

3–4 cooking apples
about 115g (4oz) caster or
    brown sugar
½ level teaspoon ground cinnamon
1 level tablespoon cornflour

2 teaspoons lemon juice
50g (1¾oz) sultanas or raisins
350g (12oz) shortcrust pastry
1 small egg
1 tablespoon cold water

Peel, core and slice the apples and put them in a saucepan with the sugar and cinnamon. Combine cornflour and lemon juice together to make a paste and then add to the saucepan. Cook over low heat until the apples are tender, but not broken up, stirring frequently. Remove from heat and allow to cool. Add sultanas or raisins and taste for sweetness.

Roll out the pastry on a lightly floured board to about 3mm (⅛in) thickness and cut into 4 circles 20cm (8in) in diameter or 6 smaller circles. Divide the apple mixture between circles, and draw up the edges of the pastry to make a seam across the top, pinching the edges together firmly. Crimp the edges together to make a neat ridge. Place on a greased baking tray and chill again.

Beat the egg with 1 tablespoon water. Brush glaze over the pasties and make a slit in the top of each one. Bake in a preheated oven at 220°C (425°F, Gas mark 7) for 20–30 minutes or until golden brown.

Serve hot or cold with cream. Try removing a small piece of pastry from the top of each pasty and putting in a dollop of clotted cream.

Mucky-mouth Pie

A traditional fruit pie from the north of England made with apples, bilberries and fresh mint. For many centuries the latter was thought to be aphrodisiac, but who knows whether northern housewives were aware of this? Certainly this pie was a favourite with their menfolk. The pastry lid is 'iced' in the traditional way, so the fruit needs to be on the sharp side. If you don't want to use bilberries, blackcurrants, blackberries, blueberries or damsons are all suitable.

serves 6

225g (8oz) shortcrust pastry

for the filling
2 large Bramley apples
450g (1lb) bilberries
a little caster sugar

2 tablespoons fresh mint,
    finely chopped

for the icing
1 large egg white
115g (4oz) icing sugar

Chill the pastry, then roll out half of it and use it to line a buttered 20cm (8in) pie plate. Prick the base of the pastry, then chill again.

Peel, core and slice the apples and cook them to a purée with a very little water. Mix with the bilberries and chopped mint. Sprinkle with a little sugar – not too much because of the sweet icing on top of the pie. Spoon the fruit mixture into the flan ring or pie plate and roll out the rest of the pastry to make a lid. Bake in a preheated oven at 200°C (400°F, Gas mark 6) for about 25 minutes, then remove from the oven and leave to cool slightly. Reduce the oven to 180°C (350°F, Gas mark 4).

To prepare the icing, whisk the egg white until very stiff, then whisk in the sieved icing sugar until the mixture stands in peaks. Spread thickly over the pie crust and put back in the oven for about 10 minutes, until the icing hardens and is very slightly browned. Serve warm with cream.

Royal Pie

In Elizabethan times a 'royal pye' was any savoury or sweet pie which was 'iced' with sugar and egg white, more like modern royal icing than meringue, which is a descendant. This particular Royal Pye is filled with mincemeat, apples and grapes and is ideal for serving at Christmas alongside, or instead of, the plum pudding. The rich shortcrust pastry was originally called 'biscuit crust'.

serves
6–8

175g (6oz) sweet shortcrust pastry
(see Chocolate and Prune Tart
page 158)

for the filling
450g (1lb) Cox's apples

115g (4oz) seedless green grapes
450g (1lb) homemade or good-quality
mincemeat
1–2 tablespoons brandy or sherry
2 egg whites
115g (4oz) caster sugar

After making your pastry, chill in the refrigerator for 30 minutes, then roll out and use to line a buttered 23cm (9in) flan tin. Chill again for about 15 minutes. Preheat the oven to 200°C (400°F, Gas mark 6) and bake blind in the usual way (see Apricot Amber Pudding, page 32).

Peel, core and chop the apples. Halve the grapes if large. Mix the apples and grapes with the mincemeat, stir in the brandy or sherry, then spoon the mixture into the pastry case. Cook in the preheated oven at 190°C (375°F, Gas mark 5) for 30 minutes.

Whisk the egg whites until stiff and whisk in half the caster sugar until smooth and glossy. Gently fold in the remaining sugar and pile the meringue on top of the pie. Put back in the oven and bake for a further 15–20 minutes until meringue is crisp and lightly brown. Serve warm with cream.

Rhubarb & Orange Lattice Tart

for the pastry

175g (6oz) plain flour

pinch of salt

1 teaspoon ground ginger or cinnamon

85g (3oz) butter

25g (1oz) caster sugar

1 egg, beaten

about 2 tablespoons ice-cold water

for the filling

450g (1lb) young rhubarb

25g (1oz) plain flour

about 115g (4oz) caster sugar

zest of 1 orange

1 egg, beaten

4 tablespoons orange juice

milk and caster sugar, for glazing

Sieve the flour, salt and spice into a mixing bowl. Rub in the butter lightly until the mixture resembles breadcrumbs. Stir in the sugar and mix to a firm dough with the beaten egg and water. Roll out thinly and use to line a buttered 20cm (8in) flan tin. Chill for 30 minutes, then bake blind in the usual way (see Apricot Amber Pudding, page 32).

Cut the rhubarb into short lengths and arrange in the chilled pastry case. Put the flour, sugar and orange zest in a small basin. Add the beaten egg and blend well until smooth. Heat the orange juice in a small saucepan until it reaches boiling point, then pour on the egg mixture gradually, stirring continuously. Return to the pan and bring to the boil again, stirring all the time. Pour over the rhubarb. Roll the pastry trimmings into long strips 1cm (½in) wide and arrange in a lattice pattern over the top of the tart, twisting them like barley sugar, and sticking the ends down with a little water. Brush each strip with a little milk and then sprinkle with some sugar.

Bake in a preheated oven at 200°C (400°F, Gas mark 6) for 35–40 minutes, until the rhubarb is tender and the pastry lattice is golden. Serve warm or cold, with Vanilla Custard Sauce (see page 207).

Blackcurrant Plate Pie

for the pastry
225g (8oz) plain flour
pinch of salt
1 dessertspoon ground cinnamon
50g (1¾oz) butter or margarine
50g (1¾oz) lard
3 tablespoons cold water

for the filling
450g (1lb) fresh or frozen
    blackcurrants
115g (4oz) caster sugar
knob of softened butter
milk and caster sugar,
    for glazing

Sieve the flour, salt and cinnamon together into a mixing bowl. Rub in the fats until mixture resembles breadcrumbs. Add enough water to mix to a firm dough. Knead lightly until smooth, and chill.

Put the blackcurrants and sugar in a saucepan. Cook over gentle heat until the juices begin to run, then cook more rapidly for a few minutes, stirring frequently until the blackcurrants look thick and rich. Taste and add more sugar if necessary. Turn into a dish and cool.

Roll out the pastry thinly on a lightly floured board. Using half the pastry, line a buttered 20–23cm (8–9in) ovenproof plate. Prick the bottom of the pastry with a fork, brush with softened butter (this will help to prevent the pastry at the bottom from going too soggy) and chill for a few minutes. Fill the plate with cooked blackcurrants. Roll out the remaining pastry to make a lid, dampening edges and pressing together well to seal. Flute the edges of the pie. Cut a 5cm (2in) cross in the centre of the top of the pie and fold back each triangle of pastry to make an open square showing the blackcurrants. Brush the pastry with milk and sprinkle with caster sugar. Bake near the top of a preheated oven at 220°C (425°F, Gas mark 7) for 10 minutes to set the pastry and then decrease the temperature to 180°C (350°F, Gas mark 4) for a further 20–25 minutes.

Serve hot or cold, sprinkled with more caster sugar and with cinnamon-flavoured whipped cream or clotted cream piled on the square of blackcurrants showing on top of the pie.

Raspberries & Cream Tart

This delicious tart recipe is based on one which dates back to the 17th century. In the original, the highly spiced raspberries were set in an egg custard and cooked in a thin-lidded puff-pastry pie. Other soft fruits like strawberries, cherries, blueberries and bilberries are successful and almond pastry is delicious, although more difficult to handle.

serves 6–8

175g (6oz) sweet shortcrust pastry
  (see Chocolate and Prune Tart
  page 158, but add 2–3 drops of
  vanilla extract to the egg yolks)

for the filling
900g (2lb) fresh raspberries
about 115g (4oz) caster sugar
3 large eggs
1 level tablespoon cornflour
300ml (½ pint) single cream
1 tablespoon raspberry liqueur

After making and chilling the pastry, use it to line a buttered 25cm (10in) flan tin. Chill again for 15 minutes, then bake blind in the usual way (see Apricot Amber Pudding, page 32). Remove the pastry case from the oven and set aside to cool.

Reduce the oven temperature to 180°C (350°F, Gas mark 4). Fill the pastry case with raspberries and sprinkle them with 85g (3oz) caster sugar. Beat the eggs, remaining sugar and cornflour together until almost white. Stir in the cream and liqueur and taste for sweetness. Add more sugar if you wish. Pour the egg mixture over the raspberries and bake in the centre of the oven for 35–40 minutes, or until the custard has just set.

Serve warm with Vanilla Ice Cream (see page 71) or cream.

Cherry & Brandy Dish Pie

Cherry pies and 'bumpers', or pasties, were baked and eaten at cherry-pie feasts to celebrate the harvesting of the fruit in the principal cherry-growing areas of England, such as Kent and Buckinghamshire.

serves
6

for the pastry
225g (8oz) plain flour
pinch of salt
115g (4oz) butter
25g (1oz) caster sugar
1 egg yolk
about 2 tablespoons
   ice-cold water

for the filling
900g (2lb) stoned cherries
about 115g (4oz) caster sugar
knob of butter
milk and caster sugar, for glazing
2 tablespoons cherry brandy
   or brandy
3 tablespoons double cream

Sieve the flour and salt together into a mixing bowl. Rub in the butter until the mixture resembles breadcrumbs. Stir in the caster sugar, egg yolk and enough cold water to mix to a firm dough. Knead lightly until smooth and chill for at least 30 minutes. Fill a 850ml (1½ pint) pie dish with stoned cherries, sprinkle with sugar and dot with butter.

Roll out the pastry on a lightly floured board and cover the dish of cherries. Flute the edges of pastry lid and make a couple of slits in the top to let out the steam. Decorate with pastry trimmings. Brush with milk and caster sugar. Bake in the centre of a preheated oven at 200°C (400°F, Gas mark 6) for 20 minutes, then reduce the heat to 190°C (375°F, Gas mark 5) and continue cooking for 20–25 minutes or until pastry is golden brown.

Remove from oven and cut neatly round the lid of the pie. Lift off carefully, and pour cherry brandy or brandy and cream over the fruit. Replace the pastry lid, dredge with extra caster sugar and return to the oven for 5 minutes. Serve hot with whipped or clotted cream.

Cumberland Rum Nicky

Small versions of this pie, similar to mince pies and called Rum Nickies, can also be made. It recalls the days in the 18th century when Whitehaven in Cumbria was one of the leading ports in the rum trade with the West Indies.

serves
6

for the pastry
225g (8oz) plain flour
pinch of salt
115g (4oz) butter
25g (1oz) caster sugar
1 egg yolk
2–3 tablespoons ice-cold water

for the filling
115g (4oz) chopped dates
50g (1¾oz) chopped preserved ginger
50g (1¾oz) butter
25g (1oz) caster sugar
2 tablespoons dark rum
icing sugar for dredging

Sieve the flour and salt together into a mixing bowl. Rub in the butter until mixture resembles breadcrumbs. Stir in the sugar. Add the egg yolk and enough ice-cold water to mix to a firm dough. Knead lightly until smooth. Chill for at least 30 minutes.

Roll out the pastry on a lightly floured board. Line a greased 20cm (8in) pie or ovenproof plate with half the pastry. Sprinkle over the chopped dates and ginger. Cream the butter and the sugar together until pale and fluffy. Beat in the rum gradually. Spread the mixture over the fruit in the pie plate. Cover with the remaining pastry, sealing the edges well. Make a couple of slits in the top of the pastry, flute the edges and decorate as you wish with pastry trimmings.

Bake in the centre of a preheated oven at 200°C (400°F, Gas mark 6) for 10–15 minutes and then reduce temperature to 180°C (350°F, Gas mark 4) for a further 25–30 minutes. Serve hot, dredged with icing sugar and with whipped or clotted cream or Rum and Orange Butter (see page 217).

Quince & Pear Doublecrust Pie

serves
8

500ml (18fl oz) water
100g (3½oz) caster sugar
1 vanilla pod, split in half lengthways
3 quinces
juice of 1 lemon

3 ripe pears
1 tablespoon redcurrant jelly
300g (10½oz) puff pastry
1 egg
1 tablespoon milk

Bring the water, sugar and vanilla pod to the boil in a pan, then simmer very gently for about 15 minutes. Peel and core the quinces, cut into 6mm (⅜in) slices and roll in the lemon juice. Using a slotted spoon to place them, poach the quince pieces in the vanilla sugar syrup for 45 minutes, or until the quinces turn pink and are tender. Allow them to cool in this liquid. Roll the pastry out into 2 circles, 30cm (12in) in diameter and chill for 30 minutes.

Drain the quinces thoroughly in a colander or sieve and then on kitchen paper, reserving their liquor for later. Peel, core and slice the pears roughly the same size as the quinces. Toss them in the leftover lemon juice, then mix the two fruits together well.

Lay one of the pastry discs on a buttered baking tray and pile on the fruit, leaving a border 2.5cm (1in) all around. Beat the egg with the milk and brush the border of pastry with it. Now lay the second disc of pastry over the fruit, pressing the edges of the pastry together well. Using the back of a small knife, knock up the edges of the pastry and make a small hole in the top of the pie. Glaze the top with the egg mixture. Bake in a preheated oven at 200°C (400°F, Gas mark 6) for about 35 minutes, or until golden brown. Reduce the reserved quince cooking liquor to about 6 tablespoons, then whisk in the redcurrant jelly.

Serve the pie lukewarm with this sauce at the same temperature. Eat with Vanilla Custard Sauce (see page 207), Vanilla Ice Cream (see page 71) or thick cream.

Walnut & Honey Tart

Walnuts have been grown in Britain for centuries. Villagers used to gather them in the autumn and make them into pies, puddings, sauces, cakes, soups and stuffings. They were also added to meat and fish dishes and pickled. This traditional tart is very rich, so serve in small portions.

serves
6–8

175g (6oz) shortcrust pastry

for the filling
85g (3oz) butter
125g (4½oz) soft
    brown sugar

zest of 1 orange
3 eggs
175g (6oz) clear honey
a few drops of vanilla essence
115g (4oz) broken walnuts
walnut halves for decorating

Roll out the chilled pastry and use to line a 20cm (8in) flan ring. Bake blind in the usual way (see Apricot Amber Pudding, page 32).

Cream the butter, gradually adding the sugar and the orange zest. Beat until well-blended, then beat the eggs and add gradually to the creamed mixture, beating continuously. Add the honey and vanilla essence, mixing to a smooth consistency. Stir in the broken walnuts, then pour into the pastry case. Arrange walnut halves on top, then bake in the centre of a preheated oven at 200°C (400°F, Gas mark 6) for about 40 minutes, or until set. Protect the top with foil if it is browning too quickly. Remove from the oven and leave to cool, then serve with plenty of chilled cream.

Chocolate & Prune Tart

Chocolate was introduced into Britain in the mid-17th century from Mexico, where the Aztecs had mixed it with honey. It remained a luxury drink as long as the price of sugar was high, and was never as popular as coffee or tea. A pie with a chocolate filling like this would have been considered a great luxury.

serves 8–10

for the sweet shortcrust pastry
175g (6oz) plain flour
pinch of salt
85g (3oz) icing sugar
150g (5½oz) unsalted butter
2 small egg yolks, beaten

for the prune purée
300g (10½oz) stoned
　　ready-to-eat prunes
2 tablespoons brandy

for the chocolate filling
100g (3½oz) good-quality plain
　　chocolate (70% cocoa fat)
2 eggs, separated
300ml (½ pint) double cream
85g (3oz) caster sugar
sifted icing sugar, to dust

To make the pastry, sieve the flour with the salt and icing sugar into a bowl. Rub in the butter, then mix to a soft dough with the egg yolks. Knead very briefly, then wrap in clingfilm and chill in the refrigerator for 30 minutes. Roll out and use to line a buttered, 25cm (10in) flan tin. Bake blind in the usual way (see Apricot Amber Pudding, page 32).

Meanwhile, make the prune purée by simmering the prunes gently with barely enough water to cover, for 5–10 minutes or until very tender. Lift them out with a slotted spoon and process with the brandy and just enough of the juice to make a thick purée (about 3 tablespoonfuls). Spread over the base of the pastry case.

To make the chocolate filling, break the chocolate into pieces and place in a bowl, set over a pan of gently simmering water, making sure that the base of the bowl does not come into contact with the water. Remove the bowl as soon as the chocolate has melted and cool slightly, then beat in the egg yolks one by one. Lightly whip the cream and fold into the chocolate mixture. Whisk the egg whites until they form soft peaks, then sprinkle over the caster sugar and continue to whisk until glossy. Fold into the chocolate mixture, then pour into the pastry case.

Bake in the preheated oven at 200°C (400°F, Gas mark 6), for about 40–50 minutes until puffed, set around the edges, but still wobbly in the centre. Serve warm or cold dusted with icing sugar and with Vanilla Ice Cream (see page 71), Orange Cream Sauce (see page 212) or cream.

Richmond Maids of Honour

These particular little almond-flavoured curd tarts were great favourites at the court of Henry VIII in Richmond Palace, particularly with Anne Boleyn. Henry is said to have named them after her when he saw her eating them while she was maid of honour to Catherine of Aragon, his first wife.

makes 18

225g (8oz) puff pastry
    (bought or homemade)
2 tablespoons quince or apple
    jelly or apricot jam

for the filling
225g (8oz) curd or cottage cheese
85g (3oz) caster sugar
zest of 1 lemon
50g (1¾oz) ground almonds
2 eggs
1 tablespoon brandy (optional)
icing sugar, for dusting

Grease some patty or tartlet tins. Roll out the pastry very thinly and using an 8cm (3¼in) cutter, cut out rounds of pastry to line the tins. Spoon a little jelly or jam into the bottom of each pastry case. Chill while you prepare the filling.

Sieve the curd or cottage cheese into a bowl and mix in the caster sugar, lemon zest and ground almonds. Beat eggs, add brandy if using, and add to curd mixture. Mix very thoroughly until well blended. Fill each pastry case two-thirds full with the cheese mixture. Bake in the centre of a preheated oven at 200°C (400°F, Gas mark 6) for about 25 minutes or until well risen and puffy. Serve warm or cold, dusted with sieved icing sugar and with clotted or pouring cream.

Yorkshire Curd Cheesecake

Make one large tart, instead of individual ones, using rich shortcrust instead of puff pastry. Omit the jelly or jam, but add 1 tablespoon currants or raisins to the cheese mixture, leaving out 25g (1oz) caster sugar. Bake for 30–40 minutes or until the filling is golden brown and puffy.

Sweet Egg Pie

Also known as Custard Tart and Transparent Pudding, this pie has been popular since Elizabethan days when the filling was made with vegetables or fruit, eggs, thick cream and lots of spices. Originally the pastry case was literally to provide a 'coffyn' or container in which to cook the custard.

serves 4–6

175g (6oz) sweet shortcrust pastry
    (see Chocolate and Prune Tart,
    page 158)

for the filling
500ml (18fl oz) whipping cream
1 vanilla pod, split in half lengthways

6 egg yolks
85g (3oz) caster sugar
1 teaspoon cornflour
1 teaspoon rose water (optional)
freshly grated nutmeg

icing sugar for dusting

Roll out the pastry and use to line a buttered 20cm (8in), 5cm (2in) deep flan ring. Bake blind in the usual way (see Apricot Amber Pudding, page 32). Reduce the heat to 150°C (300°F, Gas mark 2).

Meanwhile, make the custard filling by pouring the cream into a small pan. Add the vanilla pod and bring to the boil. Beat the egg yolks, sugar and cornflour together, then pour on the boiling cream. Stir well, then add the rose water, if using. Pass through a fine sieve, skimming any froth from the surface. Pour the custard mixture into the baked pastry case, grating plenty of fresh nutmeg across the surface. Place the pie carefully in the oven and cook for about 30 minutes, or until just set (gently shake the baking tray – a gentle wobble will indicate that the tart is cooked).

Remove from the oven and allow to cool to room temperature before serving dusted with icing sugar. Eat with fresh soft fruit or a sauce, or serve plain (don't put in the refrigerator or the texture will firm up and spoil).

Gypsy Tart

serves
8

for the pastry
225g (8oz) plain flour
115g (4oz) butter
2–4 tablespoons cold water,
   to mix

for the filling
400g (14oz) tin evaporated milk,
   chilled overnight
350g (12oz) dark muscovado sugar
chopped walnuts or pecan nuts
   (optional)
sifted icing sugar, for dusting

To make the pastry, sieve the flour into a mixing bowl, then rub in the butter until the mixture resembles fine breadcrumbs. Add cold water and mix to a dough. Knead lightly, then leave to rest for at least 10 minutes in the refrigerator. Preheat the oven to 200°C (400°F, Gas mark 6) with a large baking sheet in the oven to heat up as well.

Roll the pastry out and line a deep, buttered, 25cm (10in) loose-bottomed flan tin. Bake blind in the usual way (see Apricot Amber Pudding, page 32). Meanwhile, whisk the evaporated milk and sugar with an electric whisk, for about 15 minutes.

Remove the baking sheet with the pastry case from the oven. Pour the filling into the pastry case and scatter over the chopped nuts if using. Return to the centre of the oven and bake for a further 10 minutes (the filling will still be slightly wobbly but will set on cooling). Remove from the oven and leave to cool until just warm.

Serve dusted with icing sugar and with pouring cream.

Orange-flower Cheese Tart

Orange-flower water was substituted for rose water in some English dishes towards the end of the 17th century. Few English gardens had fallen orange blossoms to make this scented water, so it was usually imported from France or Portugal. Both orange-flower and rose water continued in popularity as food flavourings all through the 18th century, but then lost favour. Recently, there has been a renewed interest and they can be bought at grocers or chemists. Bake this tart the day before serving.

serves 12

225g (8oz) digestive biscuits
225g (8oz) butter
700g (1lb 9oz) cream cheese
225g (8oz) caster sugar
3 eggs

1 teaspoon orange-flower water
1 level tablespoon orange zest
150ml (¼ pint) soured cream
fresh orange segments,
    for decorating

Put the biscuits in a plastic bag and crush with a rolling pin. Melt 115g (4oz) butter and mix together with the biscuit crumbs in a mixing bowl. Press into a 23cm (9in) spring-release cake tin to cover the base. Place in the refrigerator while making filling.

In a large mixing bowl, beat the cream cheese until smooth. Slowly beat in the sugar until evenly blended. Add the remaining butter, melted in a small saucepan, beaten eggs, orange-flower water and orange zest. Continue beating until the mixture is really smooth. Pour into the chilled crumb base. Bake in the centre of a preheated oven at 150°C (300°F, Gas mark 2) for 45 minutes. Turn off the oven, but leave the cheesecake in the oven for a further 30 minutes. Remove from the oven and cool. Leave in a cool place overnight if possible.

To serve, remove the sides of the tin and loosen the cheesecake from the base with a palette knife. Slide it on to a plate and spread the top with soured cream. Decorate with fresh orange segments.

Manchester Tart

Also called Manchester Pudding, as its original form in the 18th century would have been made in a deep pie dish lined around the side with pastry.

serves
6

175g (6oz) shortcrust pastry

for the filling
300ml (½ pint) full-cream milk
zest of 1 lemon
50g (1¾oz) fresh white breadcrumbs
2 large eggs, separated
50g (1¾oz) butter, melted
1 tablespoon brandy
100g (3¾oz) caster sugar
3 tablespoons good-quality jam
    of your choice

Roll out the pastry and use to line a buttered 20cm (8in) pie plate or shallow flan tin. Bake blind in the usual way (see Apricot Amber Pudding, page 32).

To make the filling, bring the milk to the boil in a pan with the lemon zest. Remove from the heat and allow to cool so that the flavour of the lemon will infuse with the milk. Pour the cooled milk through a sieve over the breadcrumbs. Beat the egg yolks into the mixture, then add the melted butter, brandy and 25g (1oz) of the sugar. Spread your chosen jam on to the bottom of the pastry case and pour over the filling.

Bake in a preheated oven at 180°C (350°F, Gas mark 4) for 40–45 minutes. While the tart is cooking, whisk the egg whites with half the remaining sugar until stiff, then fold in the rest of the sugar. Coat the top of the tart with this meringue, then put back in the oven for about 15 minutes until crisp and lightly browned.

Treacle Tart

With the setting up of sugar refineries in British ports in the late 18th century, treacle, the syrup remaining after the sugar had been refined, became generally available. The origin of treacle tart may be medieval gingerbread, which was made by pressing breadcrumbs, treacle, spices and colourings together. Treacle was later replaced in tarts by golden syrup, but the name remained. In the north it continued to be popular as it was a cheaper sweetener.

serves
6

175g (6oz) shortcrust, sweet shortcrust or almond pastry

for the filling
50g (1¾oz) fresh white breadcrumbs
zest and juice of 1 lemon
½ teaspoon ground ginger
6 tablespoons golden syrup
3 tablespoons double cream

Chill the pastry, then roll out thinly and use to line a buttered 20cm (8in) shallow loose-bottomed flan tin. Prick all over and chill for at about 30 minutes, then bake blind in the usual way (see Apricot Amber Pudding, page 32). Remove from the oven and cool briefly.

Mix the filling ingredients together and pour into the pastry case. Bake in a preheated oven at 200°C (400°F, Gas mark 6) for 5 minutes, then reduce to 160°C (325°F, Gas mark 3). Bake for a further 25 minutes, or until golden brown and set.

Remove from the oven and leave to cool for at least 30 minutes, then serve warm with Vanilla Custard Sauce (see page 207), Vanilla Ice Cream (see page 71), Honey and Brandy Ice Cream (see page 74) or cream.

Lady's Tart

This 19th-century tart was originally filled with apricot preserve and decorated with flaked almonds. It had a decorative edge of small pastry circles. In this recipe, I have used four varieties of jam laid in sections and divided by strips of pastry – once the pride of housewives, who, of course, used their best homemade jams.

serves 6

225g (8oz) shortcrust pastry
2 tablespoons apricot jam
2 tablespoons raspberry or
    strawberry jam
2 tablespoons blackcurrant jam
2 tablespoons green gooseberry
    or greengage jam
milk or water, for brushing
1 egg, beaten
1 tablespoon cold water

Roll out the pastry thinly and use two-thirds of it to line a buttered 25cm (10in) ovenproof plate. Divide the pastry base into 8 sections, marking lightly with a knife. Spread each section with the different jams alternating the colours and avoiding the rim of the plate. Cut the pastry trimmings into narrow strips and arrange in twists across the tart dividing the jams.

Cut the remaining one-third of the pastry into small circles with a 2.5cm (1in) cutter. Brush the rim of the pastry-lined plate with a little milk or water and arrange the circles around the edge, overlapping them a little.

Beat the egg with the water and brush the pastry circles and twists carefully to glaze. Bake in the centre of a preheated oven at 190°C (375°F, Gas mark 5) for about 30 minutes or until pastry is golden brown. Serve hot or cold with Vanilla Custard Sauce (see page 207) or with thick cream.

Steamed &
Boiled Puddings

Apple Hat

A favourite Victorian suet-crust pudding filled with apples, raisins and spices. Other seasonal fruits are just as successful – try pears, plums, damsons or gooseberries. The dried fruit can be omitted, chopped nuts added and alternative spices used.

serves 6

225g (8oz) self raising flour
pinch of salt
115g (4oz) suet
6–8 tablespoons cold water
675g (1½lb) cooking apples
50g (1¾oz) raisins or sultanas
85g (3oz) brown or white sugar

3 cloves
pinch of ground cinnamon
pinch of ground ginger
zest and juice of ½ lemon
   or 1 orange
50g (1¾oz) unsalted butter
1 tablespoon clotted cream

Sieve the flour with the salt into a mixing bowl. Stir in the suet and mix with sufficient cold water to make a soft, light dough. Knead lightly and roll out on a floured board about 6mm (¼in) thick. Use two-thirds of the pastry to line a prepared basin.

Peel, core and slice the apples and fill the lined basin with layers of apples, raisins or sultanas, sugar and spices. Add lemon or orange zest and juice and the butter, cut into small pieces. Cover the basin with reserved piece of pastry, dampening the edges and pressing together firmly. Cover securely and steam for 2–2½ hours.

Turn out on to a warm serving plate and remove a square of the pastry from the top of the pudding. Pop in a tablespoon of clotted cream which will melt into the pudding. Serve hot with Vanilla Custard Sauce (see page 207).

Apple & Bramble Hat

Use 450g (1lb) cooking apples and 225g (8oz) blackberries. Omit raisins.

Bachelor's Pudding

serves 6

2 tablespoons golden syrup
115g (4oz) unsalted butter
115g (4oz) caster sugar
2 eggs
140g (5oz) self-raising flour

2 tablespoons milk or water
450g (1lb) cooking apples
50g (1¾oz) currants
85g (3oz) demerara sugar
1 level teaspoon ground cinnamon

Butter thoroughly a 1.2 litre (2 pint) pudding basin. Pour golden syrup into the bottom. Cream butter and caster sugar together until pale and fluffy. Beat eggs and add gradually to creamed mixture. Fold in flour gently with a metal spoon. Add sufficient milk or water to make a soft dropping consistency.

Peel, core and slice the apples and mix with the currants, demerara sugar and cinnamon. Pour a layer of pudding mixture into the bottom of the prepared basin, top with a layer of apple mixture and then another layer of pudding mixture and then remaining apples. Spoon over remaining pudding mixture. Cover securely and steam for 2–2½ hours until firm and well risen.

Turn out on to a warm serving dish and serve with clotted cream or Vanilla Custard Sauce (see page 207).

Rich Fig & Almond Pudding

Figs are often associated with religious festivals, and fig pudding was traditionally eaten on Mothering Sunday in Lancashire. Further south in Buckinghamshire and the home counties, figs were eaten on Palm Sunday. This custom was said to be connected with the gospel account of the barren fig tree. The use of figs makes this a very substantial pudding for Christmas.

serves 6

225g (8oz) dried figs
225g (8oz) stoned dates
115g (4oz) raisins
2 tablespoons brandy, rum or Madeira
225g (8oz) self-raising flour
pinch of salt

175g (6oz) fresh white breadcrumbs
175g (6oz) suet
50g (1¾oz) ground almonds
3 eggs
zest and juice of 1 lemon
a little milk or water

Chop the figs and dates, mix with raisins and sprinkle with brandy, rum or Madeira. Cover and leave to soak for at least 1 hour. Butter a 1.2 litre (2 pint) pudding basin well. Sieve the flour and salt together into a mixing bowl. Stir in the crumbs, suet and ground almonds. Beat the eggs and mix into the dry ingredients with lemon zest and juice. Add fruit and mix thoroughly, adding a little milk or water, if necessary, to make a soft dropping consistency. Turn into the prepared basin, cover securely and steam for 4 hours until firm and well risen. Serve hot with Vanilla Custard Sauce (see page 207) or with clotted cream.

Date & Walnut Pudding

A very popular pudding from the early 19th century.

115g (4oz) roughly chopped dates
1 tablespoon rum
85g (3oz) self-raising flour
pinch of salt
½ teaspoon mixed spice
85g (3oz) fresh white or brown breadcrumbs
85g (3oz) suet
2 heaped tablespoons soft brown sugar
50g (1¾oz) roughly chopped walnuts
2 eggs
1–2 tablespoons milk or water

Soak the chopped dates in the rum while you prepare the pudding. Butter
thoroughly a 850ml (1½ pint) pudding basin.

Sieve the flour, salt and spice together into a bowl. Stir in the breadcrumbs,
suet, sugar, chopped walnuts and dates, including the rum. Beat the eggs and
add to the pudding mixture with enough milk or water to make a soft dropping
consistency. Turn the pudding mixture into the prepared basin, cover securely
and steam for about 2 hours.

Serve hot with Vanilla Custard Sauce (see page 207) or thick cream.

Traditional Christmas Plum Pudding

Plum porridge or pottage was the earliest form of plum pudding and dates back to medieval times. This was made from meat, usually shin of beef and veal, stewed together with currants, raisins, prunes (the dried plums which give their names to the mixture), spices, sugar, sack, lemon juice and claret. The whole thing was thickened with brown breadcrumbs or sago. By the 19th century, meat had been left out and the pudding became more like our modern-day Christmas pudding.

The idea of putting silver trinkets and charms into the pudding probably came from the earlier tradition of the beans inside the Twelfth Night Cake, but this has since died out. It is still traditional to bury a silver coin, if you have one, in the mixture. All the family should stir the pudding in turn on Stir-up Sunday, the Sunday before Advent, and make a wish at the same time. The coin should then be pushed in, plus a ring and a thimble; the coin is to bring worldly fortune, the ring a marriage and the thimble a life of blessedness.

makes 5 x 450g (1lb) puddings

225g (8oz) large prunes
300ml (½ pint) cold tea
225g (8oz) currants
225g (8oz) sultanas
225g (8oz) large raisins
225g (8oz) self-raising flour
¼ teaspoon salt
½ teaspoon baking powder
1 teaspoon mixed spice
½ teaspoon grated nutmeg
½ teaspoon cinnamon
½ teaspoon ground ginger
450g (1lb) fresh white breadcrumbs
225g (8oz) soft dark brown sugar

225g (8oz) shredded suet
50g (1¾oz) candied citron peel, chopped
50g (1¾oz) candied orange and lemon peel, finely chopped
115g (4oz) blanched almonds, chopped
zest and juice of 1 orange
zest and juice of 1 lemon
115g (4oz) carrot, grated
115g (4oz) cooking apple, grated
300ml (½ pint) stout
3 eggs, beaten
rum to mix, about 4 tablespoons

Soak the prunes overnight in cold tea. Next day, drain, remove the stones and chop the prunes finely. The addition of prunes gives a richer, darker colour to the pudding as well as a very good flavour. Wash and dry all the remaining dried fruit and stone raisins if necessary.

Sieve the flour, salt, baking powder and spices together into a very large bowl. Add breadcrumbs, sugar and suet, mixing in each ingredient thoroughly. Gradually mix in all the dried fruit, candied peel and almonds. Stir in the zest and juice of the lemon and orange, followed by the grated carrot and apple. Pour in the stout and mix until smooth. Cover the basin with a clean cloth and leave in a cool place overnight or longer if convenient (the flavour will improve). In fact, the mixture can be left to stand for a fortnight or longer at this point. Stir the mixture every day if you decide to do this.

On the day you want to cook the puddings, add the beaten eggs. Stir furiously until the pudding ingredients are thoroughly blended. Add enough rum to make a soft dropping consistency. Spoon the mixture into greased pudding basins to come within 2.5cm (1in) of the rim, packing the mixture down well with the back of a wooden spoon. You will need 5 x 450g (1lb) basins or 2 x 900g (2lb) and 1 x 450g (1lb) basin. Cover the top of each with greased greaseproof paper. Put a thick layer of flour on top of the greaseproof paper, pressing it down well (this will become a solid paste and act as a seal both for cooking and storing). Then cover with another piece of greaseproof paper. Finally, cover the basins with a pudding cloth, muslin or aluminium foil, making a pleat in the centre to allow room for the puddings to rise during cooking. Tie securely with string and make a handle of string across the top of each basin, so that you can lift the puddings in and out of the pan easily.

Place puddings in a steamer, double boiler, or in a large pan of gently boiling water. Steam for at least 6 hours, topping up the water level from time to time with boiling water. When cooked, remove the puddings from the pan and leave until cold. Renew the top piece of greaseproof paper and cloth and store in a cool, dry place until needed.

On the great day, steam again for 2–3 hours before serving. Turn out on to a large platter. Sprinkle with icing sugar. Heat some brandy, whisky, rum or Kirsch in a small saucepan or ladle. Pour over the pudding and set alight. Bring the pudding to the table, burning, and surrounded by a neat hedge of holly. Any spirit can be used, but you will find that rum burns longer. Make sure your holly doesn't go up in smoke!

Granny's Leg

Also called Spotted Dog, this is a suet roly-poly pudding studded with currants – everybody's idea of a nursery treat. Until the end of the 19th century, it appeared as the first course of a meal to take the edge off the appetite, in the same way as Yorkshire Pudding, and any left over was served with the vegetables and meat to make them go further.

serves 6

175g (6oz) self-raising flour
pinch of salt
85g (3oz) suet
50g (1¾oz) caster sugar
175g (6oz) currants
4–6 tablespoons milk

Sieve the flour and salt together into a mixing bowl. Stir in suet, sugar and currants. Mix in sufficient milk to make a soft dough. Roll out on a floured board to an oblong shape about 20 x 30cm (8 x 12in) and roll up like a Swiss roll. Wrap loosely in buttered and pleated greaseproof paper and then in pleated kitchen foil so that the pudding has room to expand to keep it light. Steam for 1½–2 hours in a large pan or fish kettle.

When cooked, unwrap the pudding, turn out on to a hot dish and serve very hot with Vanilla Custard Sauce (see page 207) or brown sugar and melted butter.

Shirt Sleeve Pudding or Suety Jack

Make the dough as above omitting the currants. Roll out as above, then spread thickly with 175–225g (6–8oz) blackcurrant jam, leaving a 2.5cm (1in) border all the way round the edges. Brush these edges with milk and roll up evenly. Pinch the ends well to seal and keep in the jam. Cook as before and serve with Vanilla Custard Sauce (see page 207).

Snowdon Pudding

This pudding was re-named after Prince Albert when he came over to England, but this caused a controversy, endangering the peace between England and Wales. It was said very unkindly that 'a bad Albert Pudding will make a good Snowdon Pudding'. However, the original pudding named after the Welsh mountain is much older and brought fame to the hotel at the foot of Snowdon where it was served to hungry climbers and walkers. This is a sponge pudding with sultanas or raisins and lemon zest, originally steamed in a fancy mould lined with orange and lemon shapes and angelica and served with a wine sauce.

serves
6

115g (4oz) raisins or sultanas
25g (1oz) chopped angelica
115g (4oz) fresh white breadcrumbs
25g (1oz) ground rice or rice flour
115g (4oz) suet
pinch of salt

25g (1oz) brown sugar
zest of 1 lemon
85g (3oz) lemon marmalade
2 eggs
3–4 tablespoons full-cream milk

Butter a 1.25 litre (2 pint) pudding basin thoroughly. Sprinkle 1 tablespoon raisins or sultanas and chopped angelica over the bottom of buttered basin. Mix together the remaining raisins or sultanas with the dry ingredients and lemon zest. Stir in marmalade. Beat the eggs and add to mixture with enough milk to make a soft dropping consistency. Spoon carefully into the prepared basin. Cover securely, then steam for about 2 hours until well-risen.

Allow to shrink slightly before unmoulding on to a warm serving plate. Serve hot with Eliza Acton's Madeira Sauce (see page 211) or Lemon Sauce (see page 210).

Spotted Dick

Setting aside the double entendre, the contentious word is thought to be a Huddersfield term for pudding. A Spotted Dick is traditionally made with currants only, but use raisins or a mixture of dried fruits if you wish.

225g (8oz) self-raising flour
pinch of salt
115g (4oz) suet, butter or margarine
25g (1oz) caster sugar
175g (6oz) currants, soaked in brandy
about 150ml (¼ pint) full-cream milk

Butter a 1.2 litre (2 pint) pudding basin. Sieve together the flour and salt into the basin, then stir in the suet, or rub in the butter or margarine. Add sugar and soaked currants. Mix with enough milk to make a soft dropping consistency. Turn into the basin and cover securely. Steam for 2 hours, then serve very hot with Vanilla Custard Sauce (see page 207), Lemon Sauce (see page 210) or Syrup Sauce (see page 215).

Ginger Spotted Dick

Sieve ½ teaspoon ground ginger with the flour and salt and add 2 pieces of finely chopped preserved ginger to the currants.

College Pudding

Reputed to have been the first pudding boiled in a cloth, it was served to students in the college halls of Oxford and Cambridge as early as 1617.

serves
6

85g (3oz) self-raising flour
1 teaspoon mixed spice
pinch of salt
85g (3oz) fresh white or brown
   breadcrumbs
85g (3oz) shredded suet

85g (3oz) raisins
50g (1¾oz) currants
25g (1oz) chopped candied peel
50g (1¾oz) brown sugar
1 egg beaten
about 6 tablespoons milk

Well butter a 1.2 litre (2 pint) pudding basin. Sieve the flour, spice and salt together, then mix with all the dry ingredients in a mixing bowl. Add the beaten egg and enough milk to produce a soft dropping consistency. Spoon into the prepared basin, cover securely and steam for 2½ hours.

Turn out on to a warm plate and serve with Vanilla Custard Sauce (see page 207) or Lemon Sauce (see page 210). As children we loved this pudding with a sprinkling of demerara sugar and a large lump of salted butter!

Duchess's Pudding

A light steamed almond-flavoured sponge pudding with chopped nuts, peel and dried fruit.
I don't know which duchess inspired this pudding, but it is delicious and would make a lighter
alternative to Christmas pudding.

serves
6

115g (4oz) unsalted butter
115g (4oz) caster sugar
2 eggs
140g (5oz) self-raising flour
25g (1oz) raisins

25g (1oz) chopped glacé cherries
25g (1oz) chopped candied peel
25g (1oz) chopped walnuts or almonds
a few drops of almond essence
about 2 tablespoons water or milk

Butter an 850ml (1½ pint) pudding basin. Cream the butter and sugar together
until pale and fluffy. Beat the eggs and add gradually to the creamed mixture,
beating well between each addition. Sieve the flour and fold gently into the
mixture using a metal spoon. Add fruit, peel and nuts, almond essence and
enough water or milk to give a soft dropping consistency. Put into the prepared
basin, cover securely and steam for 1½–2 hours until firm and well risen. When
cooked, turn the pudding on to a warm serving plate and serve hot with Vanilla
Custard Sauce (see page 207) or Lemon Sauce (see page 210).

Rich Chocolate Pudding

85g (3oz) good-quality
   plain chocolate
50g (1¾oz) butter
300ml (½ pint) full-cream milk
50g (1¾oz) caster sugar
2 eggs, separated
½ teaspoon vanilla essence
150g (5½oz) fresh white breadcrumbs

Butter an 850ml (1½ pint) pudding basin well. Melt the chocolate and butter in a basin over a saucepan of hot water (don't be tempted to use cooking chocolate for this pudding – the flavour will not be as good). Remove the chocolate from the heat and stir. Warm the milk in a saucepan and add gradually to the chocolate mixture. Stir in the sugar. Beat the egg yolks and add vanilla essence. Stir into the chocolate mixture. Add the breadcrumbs. Whisk the egg whites until stiff and fold gently into the pudding mixture. Turn into the prepared basin and cover securely. Steam 1½–2 hours until well risen and springy.

Serve hot with Easy Chocolate Sauce (see page 202), Chocolate Orange Sauce (see page 204) or Chocolate and Coffee Sauce (see page 202) or cold with whipped cream.

Rich Chocolate & Walnut Pudding
Add 85g (3oz) finely chopped walnuts.

Rich Chocolate & Orange Pudding
Add the zest of 1 orange and ½ lemon and 1 tablespoon brandy.

Steamed Lemon Curd Pudding

serves
6

Citrus fruits began to arrive in Britain in the 13th century from the
Mediterranean – lemons, oranges, which were of the bitter Seville type,
and a few pomegranates. By the end of the Tudor period, lemons were being
imported in large quantities and used in perfumes as well as for flavouring
food. They have continued in popularity over the centuries. This pudding is
very light and a refreshing end to a rich meal.

1 slice lemon	2 large eggs
1 rounded tablespoon homemade	zest of 2 lemons
or good-quality purchased	140g (5oz) self-raising flour
lemon curd	pinch of salt
115g (4oz) unsalted butter	1 level teaspoon baking powder
115g (4oz) caster sugar	3 tablespoons lemon juice

Butter a 1.2 litre (2 pint) pudding basin thoroughly. Place the slice of lemon
in the bottom of the basin and cover it with lemon curd. Cream the butter and
sugar together until pale and fluffy. Beat the eggs then beat into mixture a little
at a time. Add lemon zest. Sieve the flour, salt and baking powder together and
gradually fold into the creamed mixture. Mix to a soft dropping consistency with
the lemon juice. Spoon the mixture into the prepared basin. Cover with a piece
of buttered foil, making a pleat across the top of the basin. Cover securely, then
steam for 1½–2 hours until well-risen and firm.

Turn out the pudding on to a hot plate – don't leave the lovely lemony topping
behind in the basin! Serve hot with Vanilla Custard Sauce (see page 207) or
Lemon Sauce (see page 210).

Steamed Orange Curd Pudding
Use sweet or Seville oranges and orange curd instead of lemons.

Steamed Lemon
& Vanilla Syrup Sponge

for the syrup
zest and juice of 2 thin-skinned
    lemons
200g (7oz) caster sugar
150ml (¼ pint) water
1 vanilla pod

for the sponge
175g (6oz) unsalted butter
150g (5½oz) caster sugar
1 thin-skinned lemon
3 eggs, beaten
200g (7oz) plain flour
1½ level teaspoons baking powder
3–4 tablespoons full-cream milk

To make the syrup, pour the lemon juice into a small saucepan with the lemon zest, caster sugar and water. Split the vanilla pod in half lengthways and scrape out the seeds, reserving them for later use. Add the pod to the saucepan and bring to the boil. Simmer until a syrupy consistency is achieved, then reserve.

For the sponge, cream together the butter and sugar with the zest from the lemon and the reserved vanilla seeds until light and fluffy. Gradually add the beaten eggs, then sieve in the flour and baking powder. Add enough milk to make a soft dropping consistency.

Butter a 1.2 litre (2 pint) pudding basin. Cut the zested lemon in half and trim off the top or bottom. Place one of the halves in the bottom of the basin, widest end downwards. Use the other half as you wish. Pour over the reserved syrup, saving a little for later. Carefully spoon the sponge batter into the basin, then cover securely. Steam for about 2 hours, until well-risen and firm.

Turn out on to a warm serving plate and pour over the remaining syrup. Serve with chilled double cream.

Marmalade Pudding

serves 4–6

115g (4oz) self-raising flour
pinch of salt
115g (4oz) suet
115g (4oz) fresh white breadcrumbs
25g (1oz) soft brown sugar
175g (6oz) good-quality dark orange marmalade
milk, to bind

Butter a 1.2 litre (2 pint) pudding basin. Sieve together the flour and salt into a bowl. Add the suet, breadcrumbs and sugar and mix well. Stir the marmalade really well into the dry ingredients, with just enough milk to make a fairly stiff dough. Pour into the prepared basin, cover securely and steam for 2½ hours. Turn out and serve with Vanilla Custard Sauce (see page 207) or Orange Cream Sauce (see page 212).

Brigade Pudding

This is a pudding popular in the north of England, consisting of layers of suet pastry with mincemeat between each layer.

serves 6

225g (8oz) self-raising flour
generous pinch of salt
115g (4oz) suet
zest of ½ lemon
6–8 tablespoons cold water
2 tablespoons golden syrup
225g (8oz) mincemeat

Butter a 1.2 litre (2 pint) pudding basin well. Sieve the flour and salt together into a mixing bowl, and stir in the suet and lemon zest. Add sufficient water to mix to a soft but not sticky dough. Turn on to a floured board and divide into 4 portions, each a little larger than the next.

Spoon golden syrup into the bottom of a prepared basin. Pat the smallest portion of dough into a circle large enough to fit the bottom of basin. Spread over a layer of mincemeat, then make another circle of dough to fit the basin. Continue in layers, ending with a top layer of dough. Cover securely and steam for 2½–3 hours.

Turn out on to a warm serving plate and serve very hot with Vanilla Custard Sauce (see page 207) or Lemon Sauce (see page 210).

De La Ware Pudding
Mix the mincemeat with 2 large cooking apples, cored, peeled and sliced.

Orange & Treacle Sponge Pudding

serves 6

for the sauce
3 tablespoons golden syrup
zest and juice of 2 oranges
2 tablespoons fresh white breadcrumbs

for the sponge
115g (4oz) unsalted butter
115g (4oz) caster sugar
2 eggs
115g (4oz) self-raising flour
about 1 tablespoon cold water

Butter an 850ml (1½ pint) pudding basin thoroughly. Put the golden syrup, zest of 1 orange, and juice of 2 oranges into a small heavy saucepan. Warm gently to make a runny sauce. Fold in the breadcrumbs and pour the sauce into the bottom of prepared basin.

Cream the butter and sugar together until pale and fluffy. Beat the eggs and add a little at a time to the creamed mixture. Sieve the flour and gently fold into the mixture using a metal spoon. Stir in the zest of the second orange and enough water to make a soft dropping consistency. Pour the mixture into the prepared basin and cover securely. Steam for 1½–2 hours until well-risen and firm.

Turn out on to a large warm serving plate, allowing room for the sauce. Serve with Orange Cream Sauce (see page 212), Vanilla Custard Sauce (see page 207) or cream.

Golden Syrup Sponge

Still everybody's favourite, this lovely pudding was made across the UK, after golden syrup was first produced in the 19th century.

serves
6

115g (4oz) butter
115g (4oz) caster sugar
2 eggs
115g (4oz) self-raising flour
pinch of salt
1–2 tablespoons cold water
3 tablespoons golden syrup

Butter an 850ml (1½ pint) pudding basin thoroughly. Cream the butter and sugar together until pale and fluffy. Beat the eggs and add a little at a time to the creamed mixture, beating well between each addition. Sieve the flour and salt together and carefully fold into the mixture using a metal spoon. Add enough water to make a soft dropping consistency.

Spoon golden syrup into the buttered basin, then pour on the sponge mixture. Cover securely, then steam for 1½–2 hours until well risen and spongy.

Serve hot with Vanilla Custard Sauce (see page 207), Lemon Sauce (see page 210) or Syrup Sauce (see page 215), or with clotted cream – particularly good for a summer dinner party in the garden.

Marmalade or Jam Sponge

Replace the golden syrup with good-quality marmalade or jam. Serve with Jam or Marmalade Sauce (see pages 210 and 211).

Ginger syrup Sponge

Sieve 1½ teaspoons ground ginger with the flour.

Mother's Ginger Pud

I remember this lovely suety pudding from my childhood. My mother adapted a recipe dated 1905 and came up with this 'rib-sticker'. If you are very fond of ginger, try adding a little chopped stem ginger to the mixture before cooking.

serves
6

115g (4oz) self-raising flour
pinch of salt
2 heaped teaspoons ground ginger
115g (4oz) fresh white breadcrumbs
115g (4oz) suet
2 heaped tablespoons golden syrup
1 level teaspoon bicarbonate of soda
3 tablespoons milk

Sieve the flour, salt and ginger together into a mixing bowl. Stir in the breadcrumbs and suet. Melt the syrup over a gentle heat until just runny. Dissolve bicarbonate of soda in milk and add to the syrup.

Pour the liquid into dry ingredients and mix well. Turn into a greased 850ml (1½ pint) pudding basin. Cover securely and steam for 2–2½ hours until firm and well risen. Serve hot with Ginger Sauce (see page 209), Vanilla Custard Sauce (see page 207) or Syrup Sauce (see page 215), whipped or clotted cream.

Sussex Pond Pudding

serves
6

175g (6oz) self-raising flour
pinch of salt
1 level teaspoon baking powder
50g (1¾oz) fresh white breadcrumbs
115g (4oz) suet
150ml (¼ pint) or a little more mixed
    cold milk and water
175g (6oz) butter
175g (6oz) demerara sugar
1 large thin-skinned lemon

Sift the flour, salt and baking powder into a mixing bowl. Stir in the breadcrumbs and suet. With a round-bladed knife mix in milk and water until you have a soft elastic dough. Form the dough into a ball on a floured board. Generously butter a 1.2 litre (2 pint) pudding basin. Cut off about a quarter of the dough and set aside for the lid. Roll out the large piece of dough into a circle about 5cm (2in) wider than the top of the pudding basin and line the basin with this pastry, pressing it firmly to shape.

Cut the butter into rough pieces and put half of it with half the sugar into the pastry-lined basin. Prick the lemon deeply all over with a skewer and lay it on the butter and sugar. Then put the remaining butter and sugar on top. If the mixture is far below the top of the basin you can add some more butter and sugar. Fold the ends of the pastry in over the filling and moisten. Roll out the remaining pastry into a circle to form the lid and lay it on top, pressing the edge to seal. Cover securely and steam for 3½–4 hours, topping up with boiling water if necessary. Turn the pudding out on to a serving dish large enough for the juices to seep out round it. Serve hot with Vanilla Custard Sauce (see page 207) or thick, fresh cream.

Kentish Well Pudding

Pack 115g (4oz) currants around the lemon and continue as before.

Guard's Pudding

This pudding was originally known as Burbridge Pudding and said to be a favourite of the guards, hence its new name. It is a very traditional British steamed pudding, made with raspberry jam.

serves
6

3 tablespoons good-quality
   raspberry jam
115g (4oz) butter
115g (4oz) soft brown sugar
115g (4oz) fresh brown breadcrumbs

2 eggs, beaten
pinch of salt
zest and juice of 1 lemon
1 level teaspoon bicarbonate
   of soda

Butter a 1.2 litre (2 pint) pudding basin and put a large tablespoon of the jam in the bottom. Cream the butter and sugar together until fluffy, then blend in the remaining jam. Add the breadcrumbs, beaten eggs, salt and lemon zest. Dissolve the bicarbonate of soda in the lemon juice, then add to the mixture. Mix well and turn into the basin. Cover securely, then steam for 2½- hours until well-risen and firm. Serve hot with Vanilla Custard Sauce (see page 207) or cream and Raspberry Sauce (see page 214).

Sauces

Easy Chocolate Sauce

250g (9oz) good-quality plain chocolate
2 tablespoons strong black coffee, such as espresso
300ml (½ pint) whipping cream
walnut-sized knob of butter

Break the chocolate into small pieces and put into a heavy saucepan with the coffee and the cream. Heat slowly, stirring from time to time, until the chocolate has melted. Once the chocolate is softened, stir until smooth, then stir in the butter. Pour into a warm jug and serve. Suitable for pouring over poached pears, ice cream, chocolate pudding and meringues.

Chocolate & Coffee Sauce

115g (4oz) good-quality plain
    chocolate, broken into pieces
50g (1¾oz) unsalted butter
3 tablespoons strong black coffee

Put the chocolate and coffee into the top of a double saucepan and stir over the heat until the chocolate has melted. Beat in the butter gradually until the sauce is smooth and glossy.

Butterscotch Sauce

55g (2oz) butter
150g (5½oz) demerara sugar
1 tablespoon golden syrup
150g (5½oz) evaporated milk

Melt the butter, then add the sugar and syrup. Stir until dissolved, then pour in the evaporated milk. Turn up the heat and beat until boiling. Serve hot.

Caramel Sauce

150g (5½oz) caster sugar
100ml (3½fl oz) water
200ml (7fl oz) single cream
100g (3½oz) salted butter

Dissolve the sugar in the water in a saucepan. Do not stir. Put the pan on a moderate heat and let it bubble away until it reaches a rich amber colour. Add the cream and take off the heat. Whip in the butter and pour around a baked apple or over ice cream.

If you want it thicker, use double or whipping cream instead of single cream.

Chocolate Orange Sauce

350ml (12fl oz) water
115g (4oz) caster sugar
1½ tablespoons cornflour
25g (1oz) cocoa powder
1 tablespoon instant coffee granules
50g (1¾oz) good-quality dark
    chocolate
2 strips of orange zest
Grand Marnier to taste

This easy sauce can be stored in the refrigerator for 4 weeks to use on ice cream or any pudding whenever you fancy. Combine 200ml (7fl oz) water and the sugar in a saucepan. Bring to the boil, stirring occasionally to dissolve the sugar.

In a bowl, mix the remaining water with the cornflour and cocoa powder. When the sugar syrup is boiling, stir the cocoa mixture again and then pour it into the pan. Whisk very well, then simmer for 5 minutes. Add the coffee, chocolate and orange zest and stir until smooth.

Remove from the heat, cover and leave to cool completely. When the sauce is cold, strain it and flavour to taste with liqueur. Pour the sauce into a jar, cover and store in the refrigerator until needed.

Vanilla Custard Sauce

6 large egg yolks
70g (2½oz) caster sugar
1 vanilla pod
300ml (½ pint) full-cream milk
300ml (½ pint) double cream

Beat the egg yolks and sugar together in a bowl until well blended. Split and scrape the seeds of the vanilla pod into a pan with the milk and cream and bring to the boil. Place the bowl over a pan of hot water and whisk the cream into the egg mixture. As the egg yolks warm, the cream will thicken to create a custard. Keep stirring until it coats the back of a spoon. Remove the bowl from the heat and serve warm or cold.

Cider Custard

2 large egg yolks
1 tablespoon cornflour
200ml (7fl oz) cider
2 tablespoons muscovado sugar
½ teaspoon ground cinnamon
400ml (14fl oz) double cream

In a small basin mix the egg yolks with the cornflour until smooth. Gradually add the cider, the sugar and the cinnamon. Pour into a saucepan and heat gently. Add the cream and whisk constantly over the heat until the custard has thickened.

Economical Custard Sauce

300ml (½ pint) full-cream milk
150ml (¼ pint) single cream
1 vanilla pod or strip of lemon peel
3 eggs
2 level tablespoons caster sugar
2 heaped tablespoons cornflour
4 tablespoons milk

Heat the milk and cream in a saucepan (you can use all milk if you prefer) with the vanilla pod or lemon peel. Bring to the boil. Remove from heat and leave to cool for a few seconds, removing the vanilla pod or lemon peel. Beat the eggs with the sugar in a basin. Mix cornflour with 4 tablespoons milk until a smooth paste. Add this to the egg mixture and stir well. Pour the hot milk slowly on to the egg mixture, stirring continuously. Rinse out the saucepan, leaving a film of cold water in the bottom. Return the custard to pan and stir with a wooden spoon over a low heat until thick (don't boil the custard or it will curdle). Strain into a jug and serve hot. If you don't want a skin to form on top of your custard, sprinkle the surface with caster sugar or cover closely with a piece of damp greaseproof paper or clingfilm.

Coffee Sauce

115g (4oz) demerara sugar
2 tablespoons water
300ml (½ pint) strong black coffee
2 tablespoons Tia Maria

Dissolve the sugar in the water by heating gently in a saucepan. When the sugar has dissolved, boil rapidly until the syrup becomes golden. Add coffee and Tia Maria. Boil for a few minutes until syrupy.

Ginger Sauce

2 pieces preserved stem ginger
1 tablespoon caster sugar
1 tablespoon dark rum
150ml (¼ pint) double cream

Chop the ginger very finely. Mix with sugar and rum. Stir in double cream and continue stirring until thick. Chill before serving.

Jam Sauce

3 tablespoons raspberry, strawberry,
  plum, apricot or blackcurrant jam
6 tablespoons water
1 teaspoon lemon juice

Melt the jam in a saucepan with water and lemon juice.
Push through a sieve to make a smooth sauce. Serve hot.

Lemon or Orange Sauce

4 tablespoons homemade lemon
  or orange curd
150ml (¼ pint) single cream

Mix lemon or orange curd and cream together. Heat in a saucepan over a low
heat until hot but not boiling. Serve in a warmed jug. As an alternative, see
Orange and Lemon Sauce on page 213.

Eliza Acton's Madeira Sauce

finely pared rind of ½ lemon
150ml (¼ pint) water
50g (1¾oz) soft brown sugar
25g (1oz) butter
2 level teaspoons cornflour
150ml (¼ pint) Madeira or
    sweet sherry

Simmer the lemon rind, water and sugar in a saucepan for 10–15 minutes. Strain to remove the lemon rind. Return the syrup to the saucepan. Work the butter and cornflour together in a small basin. Add small pieces of this creamed mixture to the hot syrup to thicken. Add Madeira or sherry, and reheat, but don't boil. Serve hot in a warmed sauceboat.

Marmalade Sauce

1 level teaspoon cornflour
juice of 1 orange
300ml (½ pint) white wine
4 heaped tablespoons marmalade
2 tablespoons soft brown sugar

Dissolve the cornflour in orange juice. Heat the wine, marmalade and sugar in a saucepan until the sugar has dissolved, stirring from time to time. Stir in the cornflour mixture and bring to the boil, stirring well. Simmer for 2 minutes. Serve hot.

Creamy Marmalade Sauce

5 rounded tablespoons good-quality orange marmalade
2 tablespoons apple juice
150ml (¼ pint) double cream

Put the marmalade in a small saucepan with the apple juice (if the marmalade is very coarse, chop it roughly). Melt it gently over a low heat, stirring from time to time. Pour in the cream and stir carefully until it is thoroughly mixed with the marmalade. Simmer for 3–4 minutes, until slightly thickened. Serve hot.

Orange Cream Sauce

600ml (1 pint) double cream
1 tablespoon caster sugar
zest and juice of 2 oranges

Simmer the cream and sugar together in a large saucepan for about 45 minutes, or until it has reduced by half. Stir in the orange zest and juice and serve.

Hot Brandied Cream

425ml (¾ pint) double cream
40g (1½oz) caster sugar
2–3 tablespoons orange brandy
zest of 1 orange

Put the ingredients into a small pan. Bring to the boil over a low heat, then simmer for 2 minutes. Serve with Christmas pudding.

Orange & Lemon Sauce

15g (½oz) cornflour
300ml (½ pint) full-cream milk
zest and juice of 1 lemon
zest and juice of 1 orange
3 tablespoons golden syrup

Mix the cornflour to a paste with 3 tablespoons of the milk. Pour the remaining milk into a saucepan and heat gently. Add the lemon and orange zest. Pour the hot milk slowly on to the cornflour, stirring continuously. Return the sauce to the pan and simmer for 3 minutes, stirring gently. Stir in the fruit juices and golden syrup. As an alternative, see Lemon or Orange Sauce on page 210.

Raspberry Sauce

225g (8oz) fresh raspberries
85g (3oz) caster sugar
juice of 1 lemon
2 tablespoons water

Heat all ingredients in a saucepan over a very low heat. Simmer gently
for 5 minutes. Rub through a sieve. Taste for sweetness.

Syrup Sauce

4 tablespoons golden syrup
2 tablespoons water
juice of ½ lemon

Simmer syrup and water together in a small saucepan for 2–3 minutes.
Add lemon juice and serve hot.

Treacle Cream Sauce

4 tablespoons treacle or golden syrup
150ml (¼ pint) single cream

Melt treacle or syrup in a small saucepan. Add cream and heat until almost
boiling. Serve hot.

Brandy & Lemon Butter

115g (4oz) butter
115g (4oz) caster sugar
½ teaspoon lemon zest
1 tablespoon boiling water
1 teaspoon lemon juice
4 tablespoons brandy
lemon zest for decoration

Cut the butter into small pieces and put with the sugar and lemon zest in a warmed bowl. Beat until creamy. Add boiling water and continue to beat until every grain of sugar has dissolved (this will prevent the sauce from tasting gritty). Add the lemon juice and brandy a little at a time, beating continuously to stop the sauce curdling. When completely blended, put in an attractive dish and store in the refrigerator until needed.

Rum & Orange Butter

Make exactly as Brandy and Lemon Butter, substituting orange zest and juice for lemon, and rum for brandy. Serve chilled, sprinkled with orange zest.

Senior Wrangler Sauce

Cut the butter into small pieces and put with sugar in a warmed bowl. Beat until creamy. Add the ground almonds and boiling water and continue to beat until every grain of sugar has dissolved. Gradually add the brandy and almond essence, beating continuously. Serve very cold with rich fruit, steamed and plain sponge puddings.

Index